Why Is God Silent When We Need Him the Most?

A Journey of Faith into the Articulate Silence of God

JAMES LONG

CE National, Inc.
1003 Presidential Dr.
P. O. Box 365
Winona Lake, IN 46590

ZondervanPublishingHouse
Grand Rapids, Michigan

A Division of HarperCollins*Publishers*

Requests for information should be addressed to:
Zondervan Publishing House
Grand Rapids, MI 49530

Library of Congress Cataloging-in-Publication Data

Long, James, 1949—
    Why is God silent when we need him the most? / James Long.
        p.   cm.
    ISBN 0-310-58750-6
    1. Hidden God. 2. Suffering—Religious aspects—Christianity. 3. Christian
life—1960 –   I. Title.
    BT180.H54L66   1994
    231.7—dc20   94-46443
                                                                                    CIP

Cover design by PAZ Design

Printed in the United States of America

94 95 96 97 98 99 00 01 02 03 / ❖DH / 10 9 8 7 6 5 4 3 2 1

This edition is printed on acid-free paper and meets the American National Standards Institute Z39.48 standard.

For my wife,
who understands
something of the silence

*What is God trying to tell us
when he chooses to remain quiet?
Why doesn't he come out of hiding
and talk to us plainly when we are hurting?
Why does he raise conflicting ideas
without explaining how they fit together?
And what do we lose
when we try too hard to figure it all out?*

Contents

*"Then the Lord answered Job
out of the storm. He said:
'Who is this that darkens my counsel
with words without knowledge?
Brace yourself like a man;
I will question you,
and you shall answer me.
Where were you
when I laid the earth's foundation?
Tell me, if you understand.'"*

Job 38:1–4

First Words: Be Still and Know

A lot has happened since I began this book a few years ago. I would not have imagined, for instance, that before I completed my work, my father would die, as well as a close friend's teenage daughter. Nor could I have foreseen that the church I love, and that has been my home for more than fifteen years, would split, becoming, as I now write, what feels like a shell of what it had been only twenty-four months ago. Perhaps by the time you read this, that will have changed. I have also faced a heartbreak so personal I cannot yet bear to write about it, nor would it now be appropriate. These experiences, of course, have not been easy. They have prompted questions for which I am yet to find satisfactory answers.

I have felt the silence of God.

And yet, I have felt something else as well. How can I describe it? It is a blend of joy and hope and confidence. For though I must honestly say that I have known God in his silence, I must tell you too that I have known that silence to be transformed.

It is a silence that is articulate.

It speaks.

This book is my best effort to explain the process. And so we will talk about "The Silence of God," for it is the nature of life to drown out his voice. We will discuss "The Voice of God," for it is his nature to reveal himself. Question, answer.

Problem, solution. But this is not enough. Where I struggle, and perhaps you do as well, is in that place where God's silence and God's voice conflict. Where faith and life clash. Where experience takes Scripture to task. And so we will consider also "The Mystery of God," for it is the nature of faith to live with paradox.

Surprise overtook me as I wrote, for I started a book on the silence of God and completed a book on the faith of his children. They are the same book, of course. What transforms the silence of God and gives it voice has less to do with God than it does with us.

The voice is there.

Waiting to be heard.

It is faith that opens our ears.

But how?

Part One
The Silence of God
It is the nature of life
to drown out the voice of God

When God's voice seems unclear,
for whatever reason,
we can cover up the silence
and fill in the blanks for him.
Or we can listen carefully
for what he may be trying to teach us
through the quiet.

"My thoughts are not your thoughts,
neither are your ways my ways," declares the Lord.
"As the heavens are higher than the earth,
so are my ways higher than your ways
and my thoughts than your thoughts."
Isaiah 55:8–9

One
Silence: The Sound of Infinity

Word came to him suddenly and unexpectedly. Through violence and natural disaster, he had lost his possessions and even his family. While still trying to make sense out of such devastating loss, a painful skin disease took away his health.

Then came the wait.

As he sat, scraping his sores with broken pottery, he wondered: Where is God? Why is he silent? When will he rise to lift this heartache?

This is, of course, the experience of Job, as related in the Bible. A story of resilient faith and the mystery of human suffering.

As the drama unfolds, there is a good deal of philosophizing and speculation on the cause of Job's calamity—the static of opinion crackles. Yet even in this forty-two chapter book, God does not speak until chapter thirty-eight. When he does, he leaves the questions largely unanswered, raising instead a few of his own.

It does not take long to read the book. In the Bible that sits open next to me as I write, the book of Job occupies only thirty-seven pages. Within the space of an hour or so you could consider each sentence of the story. Having just done so again, I am struck by the sense of relief that comes when God does finally speak—in spite of all that is not said, even though the questions remain unanswered.

In about one hour, I have relived the agony and confusion that this one man had to deal with for days on end. In that dark time, though he held on to his belief in a wise God, he felt little encouragement beyond the hope that his own death would bring relief.

Job's experience was exceptionally severe, but the emotions he felt are not unique to him. We may share similar suffering and struggle with questions not unlike his. Where is God? Why is he silent? When will he rise to lift this heartache? God may appear a mere illusion, a figment of our naïve imagination.

I remember the first time I saw a mirage. I was young and was traveling with my family from California to Kansas for a summer vacation to visit relatives. As we crossed the Mojave Desert on Route 66, still several miles from the Colorado River, which marked the Arizona border, I saw on the road ahead of us a blue, watery image, the oncoming traffic simply passing through it. My father told me it was a mirage.

It certainly seemed real. But as we approached, it vanished into the nothing that it was.

In our hurt and confusion God can seem the same: an illusion that looks promising until need presses us toward him. Suddenly, he seems to vanish, and we wonder how we could ever have been so foolish as to think the illusion reality.

But now, contrary to feelings of abandonment, isn't it possible that the reverse is true? There are those whose experience would tell us that God is the precise opposite of a mirage. He is at first unseen, yet approaching him in faith you find that he is, and is waiting.

I must say it plainly, I feel it deeply: I am convinced that God has spoken. It is his nature and his desire to communicate with us, and to do so clearly. This, certainly, was Job's experience, and though my troubles may be inconsequential by comparison, it has been my experience as well.

We can speak of God as reality versus mirage—he is true and waiting, long before we see or hear him. We can reflect on perplexing experiences and confusing ideas fueling our drive to hear a clear word from God. We can say that it is logical both to crave that voice and to be unable to hear it; he is God, after all. But for me, at least, the question persists: What does the silence of God mean? Is it just that we have not heard, or is it sometimes true that God has simply not spoken?

On some issues, at least, we must face the fact: God has said nothing. We are left in mystery. Ask Job.

Of course, it is not hard to imagine that such mysteries might lie well beyond our ability to comprehend. But I doubt it is just an issue of limited intellectual capacity—trying to fill finite containers with the infinite. Surely there are emotional concerns as well. Do we really think we could handle full disclosure of the ways of life and the ways of God? God apparently thinks not. And so we remain in the dark.

Twilight is an apt analogy of our sometimes limited insight. What is twilight? Complete darkness has not enveloped you; there is evidence of light. Yet the light is insufficient to give clear definition. Reality appears as shadow, silhouetted against the faint light. Under such illumination, your imagination (or your memory) fills in the details that your eye cannot quite define. Sometimes your memory or your imagination serve you well; other times they deceive you and things are not as they seem.

It is often the same way with the enlightenment we so desire: we are stuck in a twilight of partial answers. Our comprehension is at dusk, between the full illumination of understanding and the darkness of complete ignorance. We may know enough to see—even to feel—a problem, but not enough to fathom its depth or imagine its resolution. "Now we see but a poor reflection. . . . Now I know in part" (1 Corinthians 13:12).

God has given us only partial answers, and we may walk away feeling his silence. He has spoken, but he has also not spoken. He has given us what he considers to be enough, sometimes we crave more.

For instance, when God finally spoke to Job, after all the trauma the man had experienced, he gave perspective; he did not give full disclosure. It should be noted that for Job, in that moment, looking God full in the face, as it were, hearing him, those partial answers were enough. Not enough to answer his questions, perhaps, but enough to bring relief. When you are sure you have God's full attention—when you are sure you have *God*—answers, it would seem, are suddenly secondary.

Even so, the point stands: God's response to Job is a response of partial answers. In fact, being in some sense closer to the light than Job was, we know certain information as we read the first two chapters of Job (that personal and supernatural evil was involved in Job's test) that apparently Job himself did not know, there in the twilight, even after the fact. At the end of the book, when God and Job speak directly, these behind-the-scenes details are simply not mentioned.

But it is not just Job's experience that illustrates God's inclination to give only partial answers. Consider Scripture itself.

Taken at face value, the Bible is a document of startling revelation. Its insight into the character of God and the nature of life is astounding in breadth and complexity. That revelation is also, obviously, incomplete. There is much God has not said, a fact the Bible acknowledges when it promises a coming day in which we will know, even as we are known.

Last fall my family and I moved into a new home. Friends helped us all day one Saturday as we began to settle. We went to bed exhausted but were awakened late that night as two of our friends returned to give us the news that a close friend's fifteen-year-old daughter had been struck by a train and killed. Even now, so many months later, I still occasionally awake to the sound of a freight train in the stillness of the night, and a deep sadness washes over me. As I write this, Valerie would have been sixteen today. Her mother will join us for dinner tonight, and we will enjoy our friendship together. But there will be no satisfying answers to the still-lingering questions.

There is, however, something else.

My wife and I visited Valerie's grave earlier today. We went there to leave a gold-foil, helium-filled balloon, a simple expression to family and friends left behind: we remember, and we care. Stooping over the headstone, I was struck by the inscription's declaration. Valerie's mom had planned it with great care. It read simply:

SAFE
IN THE ARMS OF JESUS

All the questions have not been answered. The hurt has not been taken away. But where there might understandably have been bitterness, there is instead a straightforward and eloquent declaration of faith. Consider the terrifying final seconds of Valerie's life, then reread the inscription. Valerie is safe; she is held in strong and loving arms.

What allows a single mother, mourning the loss of her teenage daughter, to express grateful confidence in God, even though he has not answered all her questions? She is certain that he has spoken. What she has heard from that voice in the past—and now—outweighs what she hasn't yet heard.

I was at a hotel leading a planning retreat for my office when I received word that my father had died. We were taking a break between sessions and I was talking to a friend and colleague in the hall outside our meeting room. Harold Myra, my company's president, approached me and tenderly broke the news, then put his arms around me as tears came.

I returned to my hotel room to call my mom and my wife, and to make travel arrangements. In the quiet of that room, all that I had ever heard and believed of God rushed back to me. God did not answer my questions—doubtless, more will surface later—but I felt as though he met me in that room.

Later that evening on the four-hour flight to California, I asked myself why. Why did God seem close in spite of the mystery, numbness, and pain? God seemed close, sustaining me when I needed him, then and later, as in the past, because I was convinced he had previously spoken. God had revealed himself to be caring and sensitive ahead of time, even though the emptiness now felt cold and oppressive.

When God chooses to speak, it is purposeful. Does it not follow that when he chooses to remain silent, it is just as purposeful?

Or to appeal again to the metaphor of illumination: God is called "light," but on some issues we are left to trust him in the dark. Or he sheds only such light as seems appropriate to him, so that we will turn away from the gathering darkness and its unseen dangers, and toward where we trust him to be.

Here is the mystery of God's illumination: *Sometimes we learn the most as we first grope for him in the darkness.*

Here is the mystery of God's voice speaking: *Sometimes he speaks his mind through silence.* Apparently, in the mind of

God, silence can at times put across an idea more forcefully than words. The silence of God can be articulate.

If God's silence is deliberate, if his lack of clarity comes with purpose, certainly we risk something if we take over his communication for him or become bitter at his incomplete disclosure. Can we listen, then, in the silence of God to determine what he is saying?

"O earth, earth, earth, hear the word of the Lord!"
Jeremiah 22:29 KJV

*"The message they heard was of no value to them,
because those who heard did not combine it with faith."*
Hebrews 4:2

Two
Distraction:
When Life Outshouts God

If God has spoken, if he has initiated conversation with us, as faith claims, why do we so often experience the "lull" in the conversation, not the "talk"?

What is God trying to tell us when he chooses to remain quiet? Why doesn't he come out of hiding and talk to us plainly when we are hurting?

In view of our perplexing experiences, is it foolish even to suggest that God has spoken? That it is his character to reveal himself? What are we to do with the awkward and untimely silence of God that seems to overpower all he has ever said?

For starters, let's play fair; communication is two-sided. As one side transmits, the other receives. If the message isn't getting through, we could lay the blame on the transmitter, but honesty and wisdom insist that we look also at the receiver.

I once had an absent-minded friend who was the walking definition of "distracted." I saw him more than once unknowingly terminate a conversation with one person mid-sentence, in order to initiate a different conversation with another friend who had entered the room. Normally, we would label such behavior "rude," but there was no rude intent; he was merely distracted.

But could anyone be so easily distracted? So readily lost in his own world? One ride with him in his old Datsun put all doubt to rest.

We both climbed in, then as I buckled up, he stuffed the key in the ignition. His seat-belt buzzer sounded, with all the pleasantness of your alarm clock at 5:15 A.M. But he did not reach for his seat belt. The car rumbled to life, and we pulled away from the curb.

Today, if you ignore the seat-belt buzzer—or chime, or voice—it gives up on you and quits. Not my friend's Datsun; it was far more persistent. If you failed to buckle up, it kept buzzing. And buzzing. That morning, I said nothing, and my distracted friend gave no evidence of ever hearing it.

We are a whole lot like my friend. So distracted—by what? our cares, our prosperity, our human limitations —that the voice of God is the last thing we might think to listen for. We hear only a faint, persistent buzz somewhere off in the distance, and we wonder what it is and when it will go away and leave us in peace. The irony is, sometimes, without knowing it, it is precisely that warning buzzer that we need to hear, even long to hear.

While it may be the character of God to reveal himself, it is the nature of life on this planet to drown out the voice of God. And what is it about life that threatens to out-shout his voice?

It is the cacophony of suffering. God appears silent when life itself seems to contradict the idea of a good God. If he is capable and he is kind, it would seem he has some explaining to do. Yet we strain to hear his voice, and our listening is answered by what sounds like silence. In the face of our deep and troubling questions, his voice is dishearteningly still. Why must his answers come to us so faint and garbled, just when we need him to lean forward and speak gently in our ear? The cacophony of suffering seems, then, to overpower the voice of God.

It is the party music of prosperity. The silence of God is not just the result of noisy hardship clamoring above his voice. Our good times are boisterous too. Perhaps more so. Suffering at least convinces us that there is something wrong. In the process of seeking relief, we may get around to checking our hearing. We may, in our depression, listen more intently and thereby discover that God is not as mute as first we thought. But good times are not so courteous. They lull us into a self-involved hearing disorder, in which our concentration is so inward, so self-directed, it may never occur to us to turn down the music and call off the party. We may never get around to creating the quiet so necessary if we are truly to listen for the voice of God. And the party music of our good times overpowers the voice.

It is the static of opinion. God appears silent when so many speak for him—or speak for themselves—in confusing and damaging ways. The interesting thing about static is that we often hear it intermingled with the true signal. It is difficult to receive—or decode—what is being transmitted because of all that interference. Opinion is often like that precisely. It masks the divine signal in all the hiss and crackle of human ideas.

This static does not always come from others—conflicting signals out there competing for our attention and allegiance. Sometimes the fault rests solely with the receiver: with us. We find the message disagreeable. Sometimes we know God has spoken, but we refuse to hear. We just don't like what he has said. We find it hard to believe. How could we acquiesce to this command, or measure up to that standard? And we do something quite subtle, subconsciously perhaps, but nevertheless something clearly dishonest. We conclude he is silent, and the voice of God is overpowered through the static of opinion.

It is the channel-switching of disinterest. Sometimes we miss the voice of God because of our negligence, or our disinterest, or our lack of experience and persistence in hearing. We may even accept Scripture as the Word of God, realizing we have only this one life to master what it tells us, yet we ignore it. We grab the remote and tune in some other idea or philosophy, amusement or diversion.

Sometimes we are aware that God has spoken; on one level at least, we have even heard the voice. But we have not yet applied what God has said to our own personal, perplexing circumstances. God has spoken, but we have not made the conversation ours. We have not related what God has said in general to our experience in particular. We, therefore, conclude that he has not spoken, not to us, at least. Our distractibility and our propensities have caught up with us, overpowering the voice.

It is the deafness of human limitation. It is so obvious as to be overlooked, but we strain to hear the voice of God due to our human limitation. God's voice sends out vibrations we are ill-equipped to receive; it is almost as if we have no ears to hear. We simply cannot perceive all we crave to know. We are, after all, finite containers yearning to be filled with the infinite. So it is that God appears silent, sometimes when we most desire a clear word from him. Our inability to hear, sometimes at least, overpowers the voice.

Suffering, prosperity, opinion, disinterest, human limitations—these may begin to account for the silence of God. They add up to a partial explanation at least. Distractibility and disability may out-shout God. But his silence is more mysterious than this.

"I will destroy the wisdom of the wise; the intelligence of the intelligent I will frustrate. . . ." For the foolishness of God is wiser than man's wisdom, and the weakness of God is stronger than man's strength.
1 Corinthians 1:19, 25

Three
Contradiction: Conflicting Voices

This has not been a comfortable year to be a member of my church. A year or two ago there may have been low-grade dissatisfaction, but I'd guess seventy percent of the congregation was unaware that there was a significant problem brewing. By late December, however, a rift was widening. One month later, at the annual meeting, church felt like war. Despite efforts from outside mediation, things have gone downhill since. Allegations, attacks, and counter-attacks have rocked the church until the exodus that began months ago as a trickle has become instead a flood.

What's remarkable about the episode is not that Christians have disagreed; that is heartbreakingly commonplace. Rather, it's that the drama of conflict is being played out in a church once thought so stable. Churches and denominations routinely split over issues they perceive as having grave doctrinal import. But Sunday by Sunday, I have observed this church split in slow motion over issues of personality, leadership style, and questions of insensitivity to hurting people. The congregation has simply been unable to agree on the meaning of forgiveness and the qualifications of leadership in this situation. The church now appears at an impasse. Win-win solutions have dissolved into frustrating and embarrassing lose-lose scenarios, as the unbelieving community looks on.

We might ask, What went wrong? Why can't these Christians agree? But the experience has reminded me again of God's perplexing, seeming hands-off posture with reference to so much of our disagreement.

At first glance, God does not seem to be running his church. The decisions of belief and practice appear to be left entirely in the hands of mere humans who are out of their element, beyond their expertise. Yet both sides of this church conflict, and many others—past, present, and, doubtless, future—claim allegiance and subservience to the same voice of God. How can God so trust us mere people with his Word and his work that he would permit us to fail him and one another so completely?

Earlier this year I took a break from church conflict and from my regular work responsibilities to help with a seminar in Eastern Europe. It was our intent to assist fledgling publishing concerns in their efforts to create youth-oriented materials in the former Eastern block countries.

Like much of the rest of the world, I marveled at the collapse of communism's seventy-year experiment and at the rise of new freedoms. Unfortunately, as we have all noted, communism's fall did not bring an end to strife and suffering. Economic chaos and the climate of nationalism and ethnic unrest are fodder for daily newscasts.

I was interested in the comment of one Croatian believer who expressed her regret that fellow Christians were not doing more to seize their new opportunities. She spoke of the tendency to remain uninvolved or even to become critical of other Christians, when love, tolerance, and compassion ought to be guiding—and uniting—forces.

"Communism was sort of good in a way," she said. "It built a wall around us, and we just sat back in our comfortable chairs. There was nothing else we could do. And we got all this sympathy from the West. Now the walls have been removed, and we're still sitting here, throwing stones at each other."

Cooperative as our seminar participants were, I heard more than once of the general reluctance of different denominations to collaborate. I was reminded again that, regardless of locale and all that ought to unite us, we seem to feel so much more at home in our divisions.

I do not question the sincerity that leads to our diversity. Perhaps sincerity is the crux of the problem. We hold our divergent opinions with such tenacity because we have arrived at them out of sincere motivation. We begin with Scripture as we understand it, and wind up with widely divergent viewpoints, and we are slow to reclaim the elements that would bind us together.

My experience in Europe certainly put the local church infighting in perspective. Worldwide, conflict and contradiction are all too often the norm, whether the issues are doctrinal distinctives or matters of policy or personal piety. Give us the Bible, a document to bring us together, and in all sincerity we will find ways to splinter and divide.

Does the problem then rest with us alone? Couldn't God have expressed himself with greater clarity, or couldn't he now intervene to move us toward agreement, so we would more readily present a united front to a critical, observant world?

Unfortunately, the pattern of disparate interpretation, leading to fragmented faith, is a pattern with a history. Consider these church-splitting questions:

Does God select only certain individuals and favor them with salvation? Or do people choose their own way into the kingdom?

Once a choice for God (or by God) has been made, are these new believers safe forever from spiritual destruction? Or can sinning Christians lose their salvation?

Are women "equal enough" to exercise leadership over men? Or is there a divinely decreed order that mandates male leadership?

Is God and his church still in the business of routinely working reason-defying miracles? Or were miraculous signs given at a specific and limited time in church history to authenticate the claims of the church founders?

Christians fight over what it means to call Jesus "Lord," when and under what circumstances Christ will return to earth, and whether divorced and remarried clergy can lead the church.

People who claim the Christian title differ on an appropriate response to the homosexual community and the homosexual condition.

Christians cannot agree on the best way to govern a church, and they argue over how involved the church ought to be in civil issues.

Churches have split over how many sacraments there are and how they ought to be observed.

We have fractured over who has authority in the church, what place tradition serves, and what role the Holy Spirit plays in the life of a congregation.

The list is virtually endless—as long as church history itself. All this disagreement is important, because all these Christians point to the same document as their source of leadership and authority. You'd think God could express himself on the pertinent issues in an understandable way, open to fewer interpretations.

So what went wrong? Why is there such divergence of perspective on what would seem to be fundamental concerns of the church? Is it just our limited understanding? Our inclination to bicker? Our reluctance to put aside preconceived ideas and read the obvious truth? Or do we care too much about things that mattered so little to God that he didn't bother to express himself precisely or even at all? Why is it that the church's spire so easily degenerates into Babel's tower—that place of unchecked ambition and confused, competing voices?

These are genuinely vexing questions that rise out of the silence of God and our yearning to fill in the blanks. After all, how are we to live with the incongruities or ambiguities Scripture hands us? Do we simply ignore them? Or do we grapple with them? The frustration, as I've indicated above, often finds expression in church conflict.

Yes, in this realm of doctrinal debate, there is much about which God has remained silent, as if he would rather merely listen to these discussions of ours than to participate in them himself. Or perhaps we could view him as presenting both sides of the issue, then standing back to watch our theological fireworks.

In any case, he could have given us a tightly reasoned theology text had he chosen to do so. We must face the fact that he didn't, and ask ourselves: Why?

And we must also ask this: What will we lose if we try too hard to fill in the blanks for a God who has chosen silence—or ambiguity—over full disclosure?

We will lose our unity, of course. But how much more will we lose? The full impact of the voice of God itself?

Do you understand why I feel driven to hear the voice of God—and to hear it clearly—as we are mired in the quagmire of conflict and contradiction?

And yet, this said, God's silence in our theological confusion seems almost manageable compared to the mysteries that come when sorrow chokes us, and we therefore crave a clear word from God.

Oh, the depth of the riches of the wisdom and knowledge of God!
How unsearchable his judgments,
and his paths beyond tracing out!
Who has known the mind of the Lord?
Or who has been his counselor?"
Romans 11:33–34

Four
Mystery: A Whisper of Purpose

It came as bad news often comes, in an unexpected phone call. The voice on the other end of the line was not hysterical; in fact, in my shock, it seemed almost nonchalant. A Caring Ministries volunteer from the church was telling me that Carl and Sarah were dead. Before I could regain my emotional balance, he added: "It was a murder-suicide."

I was numb. Carl and Sarah not only worshiped with us, they were good friends. They had taken the role of substitute grandparents to our sons, since our families were two thousand miles away. We had shared meals together, celebrated holidays together, worked at the church together.

My thoughts turned almost immediately to the question, "How will I ever explain this to my family?" I knew I would have to tell them right away. The television crew had already been to Carl and Sarah's house; it would be on the evening news and in tomorrow's papers. Besides, my older son, then a junior high student, often stopped at their house on his way home from school.

I was concerned, too, because of the background of our boys. Ours was the fourth home for both of them; their early years had been traumatic, and they seemed more sensitive to loss. I had often wondered how there could be a world that permitted the kind of hardship these boys endured before they were even old enough to understand why they felt confused and hurt. Every parental instinct in me prodded me to find a way to shelter them from this tragedy, but how could I?

I left work as soon as I received the call and broke the news to my wife, who, understandably, took it hard. Later, falteringly, I tried to explain to the boys what had happened. They were grief-stricken and perplexed. They asked, "Why?" and what could I say? Upstairs in his room, my older son sobbed in my arms, "They said my birthday was next." We had celebrated my younger son's birthday with Carl and Sarah in January, my birthday in February, my wife's in March. Now it was April and they were dead, five months before the promised fourth celebration. For many months, at the oddest times, almost out of nowhere, my younger son would say, "I just don't see how a man could kill his wife."

This is not a book about grief, but I write of the experience here because it is pivotal in my quest to understand God and my inclination to "speak for him." Can you feel with me the limits of human explanation and the limits of divine information? What would you have said to my sons? Or to my wife? Or to me?

Maybe Carl was not a Christian after all? Maybe he lost his mind and couldn't handle the stress we now know he was under? Or do we get philosophical and speak of the fallen world in which we live, of God permitting things he does not truly desire? I can tell you this, I have not heard or thought of adequate answers.

When we've exhausted our supply of logical explanations and relevant Scriptures, what are we left with? A satisfactory understanding? Or a still-perplexing mystery?

The mysteries surrounding suffering and death make the point most eloquently: we live life with such limited understanding.

Three months ago we buried my father, a twelve-year Navy veteran. Yes, I felt deep and confusing emotions as "Taps" was sounded, as the rifles fired their salute, as the flag was taken from the casket, folded with great ceremony, and presented to my mom. And the finality! After friends left the cemetery, I lingered for a moment by the funeral car as my father's body was lowered into the grave, and I realized that so many unresolved issues would remain unresolved; unspoken words would remain unspoken—or at least unheard.

God has spoken. There are scores of relevant Scriptures. I trust him and love him. But I run out of answers long before I have uttered my last question.

A couple years ago I sat with a friend as he described the agony of parenting his sick infant daughter. At the time he was still trying to discover the dimensions of her rare disease. Would she ever walk or talk or see or smile? Would she live? Each new medical disclosure brought deepening heartbreak and perplexity. But a large part of his pain, he told me, was caused by partial information. If only he knew the worst, maybe he could adjust to it and find a way to deal with it. Instead, he faced the pain of uncertainty, which he described like this:

You jump or fall into the water and are surprised by its depth. You are in over your head, disoriented as you try to determine the depth. If you can just touch bottom, you may be able to push off and fight your way to the surface to gasp a breath. But what if you can't find the bottom? Then you fight feelings of all-out panic.

My friend had not yet found the bottom of his pain, and he struggled to regain a sense of equilibrium. The doctors were as yet unable to tell him just how bad things were, and the partial information was suffocating. Each new test, each new consultation brought more bad news.

Since that time he has stood at the graveside of not one, but two of his children.

He is not alone in the struggle with incomplete information. To live is to grope through a labyrinth of distressing questions and partial answers. And silent as God seems, it would be foolish to try to find our way alone, without him.

God's voice matters to me, and I am driven to understand his silence because I cannot otherwise make sense out of life. I might remain indifferent toward God, and self-sufficient, if life were not so painful and complicated. Instead, I experience things that make me crave his perspective. What I hear is incomplete, the explanations maddeningly inadequate. When I compare my experience with God's disclosure, I am frustrated by what I do not know.

God may have given a sketch of his purpose, but that is exactly how it appears: like a sketch—a rough draft, not finished art. And so I would appreciate an audience with the artist. I wait, but what I so often hear is his silence, and I am driven to understand its meaning.

*"No eye has seen,
    no ear has heard,
no mind has conceived
    what God has prepared for those who love him"—*
but God has revealed it to us by his Spirit.
1 Corinthians 2:9–10

Five
Language: Translating the Transcendent

I have known Larry since his college days. I have followed him through his undergraduate studies, his graduate work in linguistics, his marriage, and his decision to call Africa home. His intent: to spend his life in Bible translation and literacy work. Through him, I have come to understand something of the discipline of listening.

For Larry, and those whose work is similar, the object is to move into an area that does not yet have the Bible in its own language. Once there, it is his long-range goal to translate the Scriptures. But the first task, of course, is learning the language, a tedious but fascinating process of building vocabulary and understanding the structure of the language through careful observation and intent listening.

You must focus on every detail, listening to determine not only which words are used when, but also how each component sound is created. You have studied the science of linguistics, and now, in the field, you note which sounds are created as breath is blown through slightly parted teeth or with the tongue against the roof of the mouth or with the clicking of the glottis and so forth. From this observation, an alphabet slowly emerges.

You make mental notes and written notes of cultural phenomenon. You go to the market. You work in the fields. You win the confidence of the people so that they are in your home and you are in theirs. And always, always you listen.

Finally, your patience, your observation, your years of training, and your listening all start to pay off. You crack the language and begin to communicate.

In time, friendships are established and the cultural and linguistic barriers shrink further. Communication becomes more than symbols shared and understood or ideas exchanged. You begin to understand one another in that deeper emotional sense in which souls communicate as peers. And it all started with intent listening. It progressed and is maintained through intent listening.

This is how we must listen, if we are to hear the voice of God.

"He who has ears to hear, let him hear," the Bible says repeatedly. But who doesn't have ears to hear? Many of us. Most of us. What does it mean, then, to "have ears"? It means that we are willing and equipped to listen to foreign ideas conveyed to us by God, in his "language."

If we are to hear him, then, we must learn that new language.

A large part of the problem we have with God's silence is that we perceive the world through our five physical senses: touch, taste, sight, smell, hearing. We understand what it means to process information through these familiar senses, but their powers are so limited! We are not able to perceive God through any of these—not directly at least. Which may be why some people can gaze at the same awe-inspiring

Creation that speaks to us of God and his power without ever considering God. Or they can read the Bible, yet hear only human voices. They remain unconvinced of God's existence, to say nothing of his greatness or love.

We touch his Creation, see it, taste it, smell it, hear it. We can, of course, read his ideas and word-portraits of his character. We can witness his work in people and thereby see and hear something of the invisible and silent God.

But to know realities that are so much greater than the physical world, our physical senses are inadequate. They cannot carry us far enough. There are those things of God that are spiritually discerned—coming to us through life experience and through Scripture, yes, but also as if by way of a sixth sense. Our physical senses can take us only to the doorway of understanding, beyond which is God himself. It is this *spiritual* sense that opens the door and carries us through.

This is the language we must begin to learn if we are to find the silence of God to be articulate. If that silence is to speak. If we do not allow for this spiritual dimension, God will remain incomprehensible, his ways and words mere whispered gibberish.

All this sixth-sense talk can sound like so much cosmic mumbo jumbo. But the point is, such spiritual insight is rooted in objective ideas that God has communicated to us in a black-and-white, ink-on-paper document: the Bible. For that document to come to life, for it to become the source of spiritual insight that God intended—even in the dark and silent times, even in the mysteries and contradictions—we must do more than read it as we might read the *Wall Street Journal* or *Redbook*. Alongside our mental faculties, and beyond the normal human channels of processing information, must come this supernatural, spiritual discipline.

This book is an effort at learning the language. Beginning with the next chapter, we will consider ways in which

God has spoken. And yet, as we have noted, sometimes God is silent. Sometimes we face mystery and holy paradox. If we are to learn the language of God, if we are to develop this sixth sense, we must also deal honestly with the mysteries and contradictions—the perplexing experiences and the confusing ideas. And we will.

This book will not resolve those contradictions. Those mysteries will not cease to be perplexing. But as we honestly grapple with the questions, listening intently for the whisper of God's wisdom, we may begin to hear what God intends through his purposeful silence.

It is out of these times in which we strain to hear the voice of God that the greatest perception may come. They may become the doorway to a deeper understanding of the will and the ways of God. If only we will listen. Intently. As a linguist, cracking an unknown language.

If only we will have ears to hear—even in the quiet—we may find the silence of God to be astoundingly articulate.

So where are we to start?

We start where he started: In the beginning.

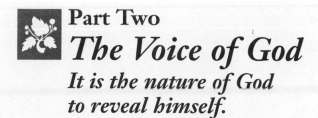

Part Two
The Voice of God
It is the nature of God to reveal himself.

*It isn't that God hasn't spoken.
He has. But something must happen
within us before we can begin
to hear his voice.*

The heavens declare the glory of God;
the skies proclaim the work of his hands.
Day after day they pour forth speech;
night after night they display knowledge.
There is no speech or language
where their voice is not heard.
Their voice goes out into all the earth,
their words to the ends of the world.
Psalm 19:1–4

Six
Creation: A Muffled Voice

"In the beginning God created the heavens and the earth."

With these ten words, the Bible begins a 1300-page disclosure of the character, will, and ways of God.

It does not defend the statement or back it up with exhaustive proofs; it just says it and moves on.

Not everyone is content to take the document at its word, of course. Some are uncomfortable with the assumption that God is, and that he started it all. And who can argue, really, one way or the other? We can't reenact the origin of the universe and observe. The statement stands, and we must take it or leave it, sketchy as it (and the rest of the Bible's Creation narrative) is.

Even Christians have not always felt content with the limited information they have received. They have wondered what to make of the language of it all; how literal is it? Or how figurative?

The religious community has argued about the particulars of creation and the natural world at least since Nicolaus Copernicus, a church administrator, published *On the Revolution of the Celestial Orbs*, in 1543, the year he died. Copernicus defied conventional, backward understanding and insisted that the planets—earth included—revolved around the sun. The earth is not the center of all things, just because we feel that we are the center of all things.

Reformation theologian Martin Luther was among those displeased with Copernican theory because of the clear statement of the Old Testament. Joshua did not command the earth to stand still, Luther complained, but the sun. Which just shows you, regardless of intellectual prowess and well-intentioned faith, blind literalism can get you into trouble. Alongside all we are so sure of must rest a healthy appreciation for our limitations and a willingness to live life with a few dangling contradictions and unresolved incongruities.

Later, after Galileo put together his telescope and started spending his evenings observing the stars and planets and sketching his discoveries, he too got into trouble with the religious establishment. In the exalted opinion of the church, the craters he saw on the moon and diligently recorded in his drawings hurt God's reputation; they depicted the heavens as imperfect. And of course, Galileo also insisted, contrary to prevailing opinion, that the earth rotated and orbited the sun. Nine years before Galileo died, the Inquisition convinced him to deny his erroneous conclusions. Stories like these remind us: we must sometimes choose between open-mindedness and empty-headedness.

Even today, there are those in the scientific community who are amused when they hear well-meaning religious people fleshing out the scenario of a young creation, brought into being a mere few thousand years ago. When we look into the night sky, we see light that took longer than that to reach us. We could say, as some have, that God obviously fashioned a "mature" Creation, with the appearance of age, and thereby hold on to such recent origins, but is it really necessary to stake our faith on the assumption that God shooed along light waves at greater than their customary speed? Are we that desperate to resolve the incongruity?

"In the beginning God created the heavens and the earth."

I am curious about the particulars but can live with limited disclosure on the methodology and other specifics. It is enough for me to embrace the statement: God did it! After all, a creative genius at work in the cosmos makes perfect sense to me, considering my surroundings.

Glancing through a magazine recently, I ran across this imaginative piece of trivia: *If the solar system were shrunk to the size of New York's Manhattan Island, the nearest star—Alpha Centauri—would be 5,500 miles away, in Jerusalem.* We know, for instance, that traveling at the speed of light, we could reach the sun in about eight minutes. Traveling on at light-speed, it would take more than four years to reach that next nearest star. At our current rate of space travel, however, it would take 100,000 years.

I came back from a day at Chicago's Adler Planetarium recently all geared up to hunt astronomical trivia. At my local library, I found this: *If we were to shrink the sun to the size of a pin head, the solar system would fill a large living room.* Let's say the living room is in a beach house on the coast of Southern California. Alpha Centauri, that next nearest star, would be on Catalina Island, twenty-six miles away. Shrunk to this scale, our entire galaxy, the Milky Way, with its 200 billion stars, would be 600,000 miles in diameter. It's not, of course, it's a trillion times larger than that.

Which accounts for one galaxy.

But there are more than 10 billion in the observable universe.

"In the beginning God created the heavens and the earth."

On this planet, there are more than 317 million cubic miles of ocean and more than fifty-seven million square miles of land, all inhabited by a dizzying array of creatures. More than 10,000 species of sponges alone. Even single-cell Protozoans are incomprehensibly diverse. Eighty thousand species have been described, but there are three times that many waiting for more exhaustive analysis.

I went to the local library for a book about butterflies. I pulled a volume off the shelf that boasted full-color photos of 2,000 species. Two thousand! I was impressed. Next to it was a book that featured 5,000. A little cursory reading told me that science knows of more than 10,000 species. To catalog the subtle differences would require 20,000 photographs.

To try to bring some order to our study of such varied life forms, we create names; names most of us rarely use. In addition to dogs, cats, people, fruit flies, and giraffes, earth is host to sea walnuts, ribbon worms, damsel flies, bog-bush crickets, feather-stars, hag fishes, spring peeper tree frogs, midwife toads, hairy-nosed wombats, web-footed geckos, sage grouse, rock hyraxes, Brazilian tapir, guitar fishes, barking deer, great glider possums, and scarlet macaws, to name but a few.

In my reading, I ran across this intriguing observation: *a column of air one mile square, beginning fifty feet above the ground and extending up to 14,000 feet, contains an average of 25 million insects.*

There's somewhere between 5 and 10 million different species of plants, animals, and other forms of life. Given the formidable task of finding and cataloging all the information, it is forgivable that the count is not more precise.

Besides all this, there is the wonder of Creation's atomic building blocks—that complex system that parallels the universe, only in microscopic miniature.

But it is not just nature's immensity and complexity that prompt wonder. Consider the marvel of its interconnectedness. From the balance of ecosystems to the interdependent intricacies of biology, Creation declares a God of order. Solar systems and atomic structures, flora and fauna—all are engaged in an intricate, divinely choreographed dance.

"In the beginning God created the heavens and the earth."

And he made people. Think about the glory of human beings and reflect on what it says of the glory of the Creator. True, people can be decidedly disagreeable, and yet they are so fascinatingly complex, with brains that out-compute computers and eyes that put manufactured lenses to shame. We can cogitate on subtle ideas and feel moral outrage at inhumanity. From where did individuals and emerging civilizations derive a sense of conscience or moral law if this were not somehow instilled by a personal Creator with such sensitivities?

Isn't it unlikely that such personal and rational creatures —with even a limited moral sense—would be the byproduct of impersonal, unthinking forces?

"In the beginning God created the heavens and the earth."

When I look up, struck by the immensity of the universe, I am reminded of Nature's mastermind. When I look around me, overcome by the diversity and order of life, I am impressed by Nature's creative artist. When I look at you, I doubt blind chance.

Creation speaks of God and God speaks through Creation. It is as though he has left signposts throughout nature, all pointing to him. He has written his name in the sky. On the face of canyons. In the intricacies of biology. His fingerprints are all over Creation. His voice can be heard in what he has made.

Creation, of course, is not a uniformly pretty picture. When you tune in a dinner-time PBS television nature special and are faced with a famished lioness munching on a gory zebra, nature can seem rather imperfect. The animal kingdom's survival of the fittest is a gruesome prospect. Besides this, people do weird things to one another, and, looking up, space is cold and forbidding.

The Bible suggests God's initial design for Creation has been spoiled. The moral collapse in Eden's garden—and since—has had nature-rending ramifications. The fall interjected sadness and death into more than human history; its corruption swept through Creation trailing all forms of disaster in its wake.

It is remarkable to read of the consequences of human behavior expressed in nature. The New Testament explains it like this: "The creation waits in eager expectation for the sons of God to be revealed. For the creation was subjected to frustration, not by its own choice, but by the will of the one who subjected it, in hope that the creation itself will be liberated from its bondage to decay and brought into the glorious freedom of the children of God. We know that the whole creation has been groaning as in the pains of childbirth right up to the present time" (Romans 8:19 – 22).

Poetically speaking, at least, Scripture paints a picture of a Creation where lions and lambs interact civilly, children have no fear of snakes, and the cycle of decay and death is finally broken. As Romans attests, nature is not yet so amiable.

If God's voice in nature seems muted, if his fingerprints on Creation seem smudged, there is good reason. Even so, nature's defects not withstanding, Creation speaks eloquently of the power and majesty of God.

"In the beginning God created the heavens and the earth."

I open my Bible to the New Testament book of Romans. Before I am halfway through the first chapter I read these words—this unembarrassed claim: "Since the creation of the world God's invisible qualities—his eternal power and divine nature—have been clearly seen, being understood from what has been made."

I fan my open Bible 617 pages back to Psalm 19 and read the same idea, expressed poetically:

> *The heavens declare the glory of God;*
> *the skies proclaim the work of his hands.*
> *Day after day they pour forth speech;*
> *night after night they display knowledge.*
> *There is no speech or language*
> *where their voice is not heard.*
> *Their voice goes out into all the earth,*
> *their words to the ends of the world.*

Creation speaks of God and God speaks through Creation. Were we transplanted into some other time, culture, and location, and deprived of any knowledge or memory of God from Scripture, still Creation would speak. But would it say enough?

It is not without purpose that the first half of that Psalm, number 19, talks about Creation and all that it declares of the glory of God. But neither is it coincidental that the second half of the same Psalm begins with these words:

> *The law of the Lord is perfect,*
> *reviving the soul.*
> *The statutes of the Lord are trustworthy,*
> *making wise the simple.*
> *The precepts of the Lord are right,*
> *giving joy to the heart.*
> *The commands of the Lord are radiant,*
> *giving light to the eyes.*

Creation speaks of God and God speaks through Creation, but what he thus says is only the beginning of the conversation.

All Scripture is God-breathed and is useful for teaching,
rebuking, correcting and training in righteousness,
so that the man of God may be thoroughly equipped
for every good work.
2 Timothy 3:16 – 17

Seven
Scripture:
A Sure & Certain Voice

I still remember my first and most intense meeting with God. I had had a vague religious experience or two in the past, fueled by emotion or remorse. This was different.

It was high in the Sierra Nevadas, sitting under the canopy of infinite stars, before a flickering campfire. Open on my lap was the Gospel According to Saint Matthew, from an old King James Bible my parents had given me as a child. I was on a week-long camping trip with my brother and had tossed the Bible in the car as an afterthought.

That night, I am not sure why, I pulled it out and read intently the whole of Matthew's twenty-eight chapters, without interruption. I read of Christ's temptation, his teaching, his miracles, the rise and collapse of his popularity. When I came to his unjust trial and grisly death, I felt as if I was there, participating in the miscarriage of justice. He was dying for *my* sins, securing through his blood *my* forgiveness.

And then, three days after death, life returned to his corpse and he left his grave alive. I closed the book, shaken by the truth of it.

Faith happened in me that night as I read, in a way it hadn't before. Christianity became more than religion, it became life. I began reading the Bible with some regularity, feeling as I read that I had received mail from God.

Early one morning less than a year later, I stood at the end of the Manhattan Beach pier in Southern California, looking out at the endless blue expanse and thinking of its Creator. I felt overpowered by the greatness of God. That morning I took a long walk along the coast, alone, but certain of the presence of God. And I prayed aloud, talking to God as if he were my best friend and was hanging on every word I uttered.

That same week I bought my first Bible commentary, an expenditure that brought a sense of satisfaction I had never before experienced. I did not feel as though I had spent money on a book; I felt as though I had invested in my own future. This conviction was born out of the discovery of God's ideas—a deeper sense of their meaning—as expressed in Scripture. The acquisition of books that encouraged my new faith became a passion.

Within less than a year, I had developed a zeal to know God that has continued and deepened over the years. Its genesis was that High Sierra experience when, I remain convinced, God met me as I read his book.

My view of Scripture has changed over the years, however, and it is that change that I feel a particular sense of urgency to write about now. I did not realize it at the time, but early in my Bible-reading experience, I was, in a sense, editing the Bible as I read—filtering out some of God's ideas, because I found them boring or bewildering, while focusing on others for their instant inspirational quality. I read the Bible in a highly selective manner, hunting devotional zingers

—divine one-liners—that would carry me through the day. I found myself gravitating toward the Psalms, the Gospels, and the New Testament letters. Occasionally, I would venture into more confusing Old Testament territory, and sometimes my quest was rewarded. A catchy phrase like Jeremiah's "Call unto me and I will answer thee and show thee great and mighty things which thou knowest not," was to me the homiletic equivalent of a political sound-bite. A single, accessible, memorable concept I could carry with me through the day.

I am not disparaging reading the Bible devotionally, highlighting phrases that seem to us first highlighted by God himself as we read. I am not even saying that my approach to the Bible was wrong at that stage in my life and Christian pilgrimage. I feel confident that God was pleased that I felt his book worthy of attention. That, after all, is why he gave it; so that we would find in it a source of wisdom and help from him—that we would hear his voice ringing in our ears as we read.

However, I remember one afternoon suddenly realizing that I felt impatient with the Bible. I had started out reading an Old Testament book; I do not recall which one, one of the so-called Minor Prophets, I think. It was one of those books between Psalms and Matthew that never seems to get its fair share of attention. I had started reading and noticed my mind was wandering. Next I noticed myself stumbling over those ridiculously cumbersome, unpronounceable words. I found, too, that I could not follow what was being said; I just did not have enough background information, I suppose. Then I began skimming the lines, looking for a break in all that dull talk. My time would not be wasted if I could find one of those little, clever phrases tucked away amid the other stuff. If I could just find some quote with devotional handles on it.

I found nothing.

I closed the book and set it aside, frustrated. That's when it hit me. *I am impatient with the Bible.* I would never have said, "Why is so much of it so worthless," but I think that's how I felt.

That bothered me later, because I realized that without focusing on it, I had often felt that way. That was what had frustrated all my failed read-through-the-Bible attempts. How could I bring myself to read every word, without feeling that I was wasting my time on Leviticus, for instance. My wife had a doctor once who, with a sly smile, recommended reading Leviticus as a cure for insomnia. I felt a little guilty admitting it, but I could relate to that.

My attitude toward the neglected Scriptures began to brighten, however, when I honestly voiced what I had silently wondered. I took my own question seriously—*as* a question, not an accusation or a slur: Why *is* this stuff in the Bible? What's the point? In time, those questions transformed my understanding of God.

Something else was happening simultaneously: my reasons for reading Scripture began to broaden. What drove me to the Bible before was a craving for a devotional high. I was propelled along by the enthusiasm of a new friendship. I had little agenda to my Bible study beyond getting better acquainted. The ah-ha sensation that came with the discovery of those devotional one-liners served me well. It fed my appetite to know God.

As my faith continued to grow and life raised tougher issues, my motivation in reading changed; in some ways, at least, I would say it deepened. I didn't appreciate God any less, nor did I devalue our time together in that book. But I began to notice points of tension and incongruity between my faith as I understood it and life as I experienced it. And so I looked to Scripture for answers to increasingly complex and disturbing questions.

What I found was that the whole of Scripture spoke to my questions more effectively and honestly than my out-of-context, selective, editorial reading. My haphazard approach, merely lifting devotional slogans out of context, led me to suppress the voice of God by choosing to ignore so much of what he was saying.

There was a scope to God's ideas that I had not fully appreciated before, because I had cut myself off from the flow and the breadth of his expression. It was as though I had been carrying on a conversation with God, but walking in and out of the room as he continued to talk.

I missed things.

Now, along with all the fascinating details I discovered, major themes began to emerge. The process was gradual, of course, and it required supplemental reading and study on the history, geography, and culture of the Bible lands. Certain sections of the Bible still confused or even disturbed me. I readily admit: you must read the Old Testament's historical books, for instance, with their seemingly endless genealogies or detailed and peculiar rituals, with a different mind-set than you do the book of Psalms. But you must read them. It is both unwise and rude to do otherwise; after all, they constitute a great deal of God's conversation.

In time, as my approach changed, I realized that I was hearing something slightly different in my reading. It was still the voice of God, but it was more richly articulated.

Even so, it is fair to ask, why this preoccupation with historical detail and cultural oddities, in contrast, let's say, to simple religious sayings, self-help instruction, or dense, mystical philosophizing? As you move through the Bible, you can read a lot of paragraphs before stumbling upon those intermittent devotional capsules. This has led me to conclude that the Bible was never intended to be strictly an inspirational book, as we have come to think of inspirational books—collections of "lofty thoughts." It is far deeper than that, though its depth comes to us at times in the context of earthy, historical narrative or, in the case of prophecy, bizarre futuristic symbolism.

It's fine to make these observations, but for me, at least, the question persists: Why? Why is the Bible so preoccupied with history?

Perhaps it is to illustrate for us that one life can make a difference. Read the Bible, including the neglected Scriptures. God works through individuals to change the course of history. And so Noah builds an ark, Moses leads an exodus, David rules a nation, Daniel interprets a dream, Mary raises a savior —these things carefully related in a context of credible historical detail and authentic cultural peculiarities.

In every time and culture, individuals matter. If the Bible's historical books constitute God's normal pattern, he loves to bring individuals center-stage to share the spotlight with him.

God has shaped history through available people. He still does so, and wants us to know it. He will gladly use you. Or me.

Why the Bible's preoccupation with history? To tell us that God is not outside the circle of our experience; he is at our side in the middle of it, revealing himself.

To convey inspiration through devotional slogans is fine; it has its place. We will cling to words that have devotional import, certainly; such words will get us through the days of adversity. But the Bible's focus on history and cultural specifics reminds us that God is engaged in life with us, on the forefront of our conflict and heartache, not cut off from it just because he is eternal, unbound by time's restraints.

He works with us in the context of our history. The experiences that bring us joy, and the circumstances that lead us into depression, all come with purpose. In every moment, as time moves toward eternity (or exists side by side with it), God raises his voice to be heard or lowers it so we will listen.

Why is the Bible so preoccupied with history? God wants us to know that at each stage in human experience, he has expressed his will and his ways, with ever-expanding clarity and richness. The Bible is the story of God's love for people and his drive to communicate with them—his passion to make himself known.

He spoke through Creation; he spoke with prophets who relayed his words to others; he disclosed his plans through dreams and visions; he illustrated his ways and foreshadowed the coming Christ through ritual, ceremony, law. He asked a nation to pass on his message from generation to generation and from nation to nation through carefully guarded oral traditions. He breathed his words and ideas through the minds of people selected by him to write them down and pass them on.

"In the past God spoke to our forefathers through the prophets at many times and in various ways, but in these last days he has spoken to us by his Son" (Hebrews 1:1–2).

You might say that it has been God's intense desire that no one would reach the end of human history, then stand before him as a stranger.

In the beginning was the Word, and the Word was with God, and the Word was God. . . . The Word became flesh and made his dwelling among us. We have seen his glory, the glory of the One and Only, who came from the Father full of grace and truth.
John 1:1, 14

Eight
Christ: The Word Became Flesh

I suppose the problem started at the Fourth of July fireworks—my best guess. But some time or other a sick mosquito found me—and a few weeks later my brain became inflamed and started to swell. The viral infection, which can vary greatly in severity, is called encephalitis. It made its presence known to me by the onset of the most severe and persistent headache I have ever experienced—a sensation of pain, pressure, and dizziness. It felt like something within my head was suddenly expanding, running out of room in the process.

After a week at Estes Park, my family and I were en route to Denver, where we would spend a few days with a college friend and her husband. My wife was at the wheel; I had the map out and was navigating. But as the headache worsened, it became difficult to hold my head upright. By the time we arrived at our friend's home, the pressure and dizziness had so increased that it was a challenge to follow conversation.

That night, between ineffectual doses of Tylenol, I checked my watch, trying to hurry along the morning. By my estimate, hours would pass, but the clock would tell me only thirty minutes had elapsed. I would sink back on my pillow, then finding the pillow painful, would sit up again. In those moments of discomfort, I prayed the only prayer I felt capable of praying. It was reverent, desperate, and, in a sense I suppose, effective. It was also a single word:

"Jesus."

I prayed the prayer repeatedly that night, softly, and I am not embarrassed to say, pleadingly.

"Jesus."

Early the next morning I was taken to the hospital. After the usual battery of tests, plus a CAT scan and a spinal tap, the neurologist gave me the diagnosis, and let me know what we'd be doing next: nothing. The no-cure virus simply needed time to spend itself.

After a week in the hospital (I felt worse the day I was discharged than the day I was admitted), we started the 1,000-mile trek home, my wife driving, my oldest son beside her to keep her company. My younger son, who had cried almost non-stop for the past five days, spent the trip home at my side. The two of us were spread out on an air mattress and sleeping bag—spread out, that is, as much as our cramped and loaded '79 Pinto wagon would permit. (During that return trip, our last $200 was stolen out of our motel room.)

It was more than a year before I was back to my full schedule. Even the pine needles falling off the Christmas tree five months after my hospitalization would wake me, as I slept fitfully in the living room recliner.

During that time, my mind returned again and again to that one-word prayer, all I felt capable of voicing that long night in Colorado, when encephalitis taught me what the word *headache* really means. As the pain increased that first night, it forced one word out of my mouth, the name of my best friend.

"Jesus."

It fascinated me that though the prayer seemed so in-
articulate, and though it did not result in healing or even in
the lessening of my discomfort, it did impart an inner calm
and confidence. I cannot honestly say I fully understand
what happened as I prayed that night. It was for me an
intense spiritual experience: thinking his name, forming the
word, voicing it, knowing that it was heard. Yes, that, of
course, is why comfort came to me: I was convinced that
he heard me as clearly as did my concerned wife, awake at
my side.

"Jesus."

At this moment as I write, remembering, my mind fills
with a wonder that feels like holiness. And I am amazed
again that it is possible to speak of Jesus in this way: as
someone real—transcendent, yet close; majestic, yet intimate; powerful, yet caring.

Who is Jesus?

As I read the Gospels, an image of a unique Jesus
emerges. I see in him a man who is fully human, yet simultaneously so much more. Human, certainly, yet unlike any I
have known.

Startlingly—if it is not too familiar—the story of Jesus
does not reach its conclusion with his death, or even with
the earth-rocking climax that is his resurrection. No, even
there we are reading the early chapters in a story that continues, unendingly. So it is that a quarter-century after the
death of Jesus, he is described like this: "He is the image of
the invisible God, the firstborn over all creation. For by him
all things were created: things in heaven and on earth, vis-
ible and invisible, whether thrones or powers or rulers or
authorities; all things were created by him and for him. He
is before all things, and in him all things hold together. And
he is the head of the body, the church; he is the beginning and
the firstborn from among the dead, so that in everything he

might have the supremacy. For God was pleased to have all his fullness dwell in him" (Colossians 1:15–19).

Who is Jesus?

When the New Testament sets out to describe his excellence above all that had preceded him, similar words are employed. "In the past God spoke to our forefathers through the prophets at many times and in various ways, but in these last days he has spoken to us by his Son, whom he appointed heir of all things, and through whom he made the universe. The Son is the radiance of God's glory and the exact representation of his being, sustaining all things by his powerful word" (Hebrews 1:1–3).

Who, then, is Jesus? If we will accept Scripture's words as authoritative, he is the creator and sustainer of the universe. He is the theme and fulfillment of history. He is the final and most complete revelation of God, because he is himself God.

In view of all this, it is understandable that Jesus would be reverenced; that we would find him worthy of worship. It is remarkable that we would also find him approachable. Except, who is Jesus?

The words above paint him as majestic and transcendent. The words that follow depict him as I have also known him to be: intimate and caring. "Since we have a great high priest who has gone through the heavens, Jesus the Son of God, let us hold firmly to the faith we profess. For we do not have a high priest who is unable to sympathize with our weaknesses, but we have one who has been tempted in every way, just as we are—yet was without sin. Let us then approach the throne of grace with confidence, so that we may receive mercy and find grace to help us in our time of need" (Hebrews 4:14–16).

We receive mercy, we find grace to help us, even if the most articulate prayer we can express is simply his name:

"Jesus."

As I write, I am thinking of the silence of God and the voice of God. I am aware of the mysteries I cannot plumb and the contradictions I cannot reconcile. But so much of what would perplex me is dispelled as I reflect on God's most clear word:

"Jesus."

Think for a moment of all he said and all he did. Consider all he is. God's silence is suddenly filled with voice and the voice with insight. The questions do not all evaporate; the mysteries do not all resolve; the contradictions do not all reconcile. But all this unknown is contextualized. It is given perspective. As I merely think of Jesus, it is as if God speaks, framing in my mind ideas about himself, answers to many of my questions, fulfillment to much of my yearning.

That painful night in Colorado when my prayers were limited to that two-syllable name—"Jesus"—I did not feel like theologizing my experience. In a sense, though, that is what I did. In reminding myself of Jesus (and reminding him of me), I was not invoking his name as a charm. There was, I believe, some mystical connection with him, difficult to fathom, impossible to explain. But principally, that prayer did this: it called to mind all I knew and believed of God, and expressed it in the limitless, succinct name: "Jesus." I would not have had the energy or powers of concentration to describe it then, but hearing my voice verbalizing his name as a prayer brought comfort, not only because he heard me, but because I heard him. In his name. That name reminded me of the character and nature of the one to whom I had previously committed my life.

Now, as then, when I think of Jesus, I hear the voice of God. When I think of Jesus, for instance, God's voice tells me he is approachable. He has come out in the open and revealed himself. He can be known.

What astounds me is that the perfect revelation of who God is and what he is like was not some immense demonstration, filling the universe. For this ultimate display of who God is, God cloistered himself in the capsule of humanity. The creator God was at home in the uterus of Mary, his mother. The all-knowing God grew in wisdom and stature, as a child, an adolescent, an adult. The sovereign God was misunderstood, repudiated, and rejected. The majestic God suffered in humiliation. The eternal God chose a life span less than half that of my father.

An infinite God could understand me perfectly without these experiences; but I know that he understands me—I feel it—because of them.

When I see the length he went to, in love, because he wanted to reach me, I know that I can now reach him. No one is outside the scope of his care. Prostitutes, traitors, outcasts, crazed demoniacs all find common ground with sincere religionists and upstanding citizens. Faith puts us on equal footing.

When I say the name of Jesus, or when I hear it, then, I picture God revealing himself and inviting me to know him. And yet, that name not only suggests disclosure, it also calls to mind mystery, for when I think of Jesus, God's voice tells me that he does not necessarily expect to be understood.

When I say the name of Jesus, or hear it, then, I picture a God of mystery as well as disclosure. To pray to this God, particularly when distressed, is to acknowledge him as both: a God of secret things and a God of revealed purpose.

It may be God's passion to reveal himself, but he knows we may be hesitant or unable to receive the truth. I cannot read the Gospels without sensing the limitations of language, of mind, of emotion, and certainly the limitations of faith. Jesus expressed what sounds like frustration when his friends were "dull of hearing" and "slow to understand." The disciples did not pick up on his repeated references to his own death and resurrection, for example; it would seem that they heard what they wanted to hear or what they found themselves capable of absorbing. They recognized that Jesus spoke with authority, but that did not mean they always connected with the gist of his message. And so, even Christ, it seems, could not put across every one of his ideas understandably; his listeners simply could not receive it all.

What I find truly remarkable, however, is that Jesus sometimes appears quite comfortable being misunderstood. When I was a kid, the Sunday school people explained that Jesus told parables to make his ideas more easily understood. When I got a bit older I discovered that he told parables to confuse close-minded people (Matthew 13:13–14). He was even unflappable when a symbolic reference to eating his flesh and drinking his blood was mistaken by perplexed listeners as a reference to cannibalism or something else equally weird (John 6). And the night of his trial he refused even to speak to Herod (Luke 23:8–9).

Jesus said: "I will utter things hidden since the creation of the world" (Matthew 13:35).

He also said, "I praise you, Father, Lord of heaven and earth, because you have hidden these things from the wise and learned, and revealed them to little children. Yes, Father, for this was your good pleasure" (Matthew 11:25–26).

Why, for instance, would Jesus so often work miracles then, yet now in our experience more often withhold them? It's not just a question of faith. What faith would lay claim to, life often denies.

It is not that I question God's facility with the miraculous, but observe: the undeserving often fare better than the innocent.

That Jesus performed even one miracle suggests his superiority over circumstance. That he would withhold even one miracle hints at the mystery that colors his purpose. This is perplexing, contradictory; I crave disclosure. Yet the contradiction comes with intent, and I trust the Mind that holds the mystery. Faith may not lift the burden of suffering, but faith

does tell me: though God's purpose may differ from my pref-
erence, there is purpose, not caprice.

Jesus said, "In this world you will have trouble. But take
heart! I have overcome the world" (John 16:33). In that
statement is mystery; in that declaration is purpose.

When I think of Jesus, God's voice tells me that he is here
for me, even in the confusion. I was reading the words of Jesus
yesterday and was struck by the unqualified promise, "I will
not leave you comfortless." In the context, he was promising
another comforter, the Holy Spirit, who would never leave us
(John 14). But take the statement at face value. Realize what it
says of the nature of God. In the darkest of our times, when
sorrow or pain leave us in mystery, what is God's voice telling
us, at the very least? Questions may remain unanswered, contradiction may go unresolved, but God says, "I will not leave
you comfortless."

And if the most articulate prayer we can manage is the
simple, two-syllable name, "Jesus," still all that he is will be
there to answer.

The Spirit searches all things, even the deep things
of God. . . . The man without the Spirit does not accept
the things that come from the Spirit of God, for they are
foolishness to him, and he cannot understand them,
because they are spiritually discerned.
1 Corinthians 2:10, 14

Nine
Spirit: Inside Interpreter

As I write, relief efforts are just beginning to pour into southern Florida, following the destruction brought by Hurricane Andrew only a week ago. Today's newspaper outlines the heartache as well as the determination, as people contemplate a new beginning in the wake of billions of dollars of destruction. Among the 180,000 left homeless, one family spoke for the many. Painted on what's now left of a house in Homestead, Florida, was the plea: "Please don't forget us, we're still alive."

Isn't that so often our cry also to God, painted across our flagging faith? "Please don't forget us, we're still alive." In our hardship, where is the reassuring voice of God?

Adjacent to this story on the paper's front page I read of ethnic violence in Bosnia. A single howitzer shell falls into the capitol city's marketplace Sunday morning, killing fifteen, injuring scores of others, ravaging recent peace initiatives.

Page one tells it all—life on the troubled planet. Read of white supremacists sequestered in Idaho, of Somalian relief efforts thwarted by black market thieves, of Iraqi forces contemplating a ground offensive against Shiite rebels, of job woes and economic distress in America.

A day passes, the headlines change. But the mood is the same. Human distress continues into the future as it has been in the past. And the voice of God grows faint.

"I will not leave you comfortless," Christ said. But how are we to connect with this comfort? How are we to hear God's voice?

At noon I take a table alone at a restaurant near my office. Without deliberately eavesdropping I hear heartache at the booth behind me and at the table to my left. Behind me, a marriage is disintegrating. To my left, a mother and her adult daughter frame strategies to confront an alcoholic, abusive father.

In the context of mind-blurring stress, what does it mean, this promise from Christ, that we will not be left comfortless?

It's not just tragedy that prompts the question. Sometimes it's tedium. A few hours ago my recently widowed mother called to tell me about the nuisance of a broken, outdoor water faucet. With water spraying from the pipe, she hunts a shut-off valve, which, naturally, won't budge. A well-intentioned neighbor arrives with a pipe wrench and shuts off not the water, but the gas. He corrects his mistake, but now the pilots indoors must be relit. My mother, not wishing to impose further, sends the neighbor home; she can handle a few pilot lights. But now, how did Derrell light the floor furnace? And only after hours of ice cold hot water does she realize there's another appliance that needs attention. A day passes before a representative from the gas company arrives to restart the water heater. In the process, he lets my mom know that one of my dad's do-it-yourself projects needs to be undone; it's hampering airflow around the appliance.

These are not major traumas, but they represent the obnoxious tedium that so often follows loss and adds up to stress. All it takes is the sheer monotony of everyday minor hassles to make Christ's promised comfort seem distant and elusive.

Where is the voice of God in the clamor of challenging life?

I write of difficulties I have endured—sickness, grief, and confusion—and I tell you I have found God close. It is true. Yet I have not always felt his nearness; I too know what it is to feel aggravation at his silence. And besides this, I cannot say what hardship I may face even tomorrow. I do not know the future, and the past has made me skeptical of those who guarantee a placid voyage in return for buoyant faith.

And yet, Christ did promise peace and comfort in the worst of circumstances, in the darkest of experiences.

"I will not leave you comfortless," he said.

These are remarkable words for Christ to say to his friends mere hours before he himself would cry out, "My God, my God, why have you forsaken me?"

In fact, those words, "I will not leave you comfortless," have also been translated, "I will not leave you as orphans" (John 14:18). Yet isn't that the feeling he expressed from the cross less than twenty-four hours later, the feeling of being left alone in the universe, orphaned?

Jesus promised his friends "I will not leave you comfortless" because comfort is what he knew they soon would need. I am convinced, however, that Jesus also knew that his friends would not always feel that comfort, even though it would be there for them.

Jesus himself demonstrated that irony. The same night he promised such comfort, he said, "A time is coming, and has come, when you will be scattered, each to his own home. You will leave me all alone. Yet I am not alone, for my Father is with me" (John 16:32). This was the source of his comfort: the Father would not desert him. Within hours, though, circumstances changed, and his feelings were swept along with the change. And he said, in anguish, "My God, my God, why have you forsaken me?"

There is, of course, deep theological mystery behind these contrasting statements: "My Father is with me," "My God, why have you forsaken me?" I do not wish to diminish the unimaginable—and unique—agony that was Christ's, sinless, yet dying with the weight of our sins pressing upon him. I do wish to stress that Christ understands the conflicting emotions life brings; he has himself experienced such perplexity.

Like Christ, we crave the Father's comfort and receive it; yet also like Christ, we may struggle at times with feelings of abandonment. Though close, God may seem distant. Though God will never leave us, we may feel forsaken. Though we have been welcomed into the family of God, we may feel orphaned.

In distress Christ spoke. "My God, my God, why have you forsaken me?" Though he asks why, he addresses the question with intimacy and confidence, not with fist-shaking unbelief.

"My God."

"My God."

I may wrestle suffocating doubts. I may question the purpose of God. Yet I cling to the confident affirmation. In the worst of experiences, in the darkest of circumstances, he remains:

"My God."

"My God."

I link confidence and "belonging" with the darkness of fear and pain, because this is precisely how the promise of Christ came to us. "I will not leave you comfortless," he said, while telling them of coming times of the deepest darkness.

As his last hours unfold the night of his arrest, Christ speaks of his betrayal, his denial, his death, and his future beyond death. He warns his friends they will face hatred, persecution and turmoil, yet he urges love and promises peace, comfort, even joy.

Relive Christ's final hours before death. Picture yourself as part of his inner circle. Hear what seem to be his final words to you. Feel the apprehension spreading through you, the tightening in your chest, sorrow numbing your mind. You can scarcely follow what he is telling you, you are so gripped with fear and confusion. Yet you grab hold of certain of his words, coming to you as if through a thick mist—you grab hold and hang on.

"I will not leave you comfortless."

"I will not leave you comfortless."

That was his promise. How did he intend to achieve it? And what does this tell us about the voice of God?

Picture again Christ's last night with his friends—with you. As the evening wears on, his intensity fills you with foreboding. He interrupts the evening meal to predict his betrayal. He rebuffs Peter's expression of loyalty: "Will you really lay down your life for me? I tell you the truth, before the rooster crows, you will disown me three times!" (John 13:38). In contrast, his next words reassure: "Do not let your hearts be troubled" (14:1). Throughout the evening, he speaks repeatedly of death, and though one could hardly say he sounds morbid, you feel already the first pangs of grief. He says, "I will ask the Father, and he will give you another Counselor, the Spirit of truth, to be with you forever" (14:16). But you do not want another Counselor, you want him!

He speaks of peace and offers reassurance, but it is so hard to hear good news with bad news still ringing in your ears.

Finally, he spells it out even more plainly: "Because I have said these things, you are filled with grief. But I tell you the truth: It is for your good that I am going away. Unless I go away, the Counselor will not come to you, but if I go, I will send him to you" (16:6–7).

Every once in awhile as I read Scripture, I am stunned by the voice of God. It is this precisely which stuns me now: "It is for your good that I am going away." How could it possibly be good for Jesus to go away?

I have often imagined what it must have been like to have Jesus as a close friend. Even many who refuse the label—"Christian"—are impressed with Jesus. And for good reason. Consider what he said; consider what he was like. His teachings elevated moral standards to unprecedented heights. He moved through life radiating an invincible tenderness that drew children, and set the hurting at ease. He faced death resolute, with a determination and purpose that put him in command of what could have been considered his ultimate failure, yet proved to be his greatest success.

How can there be anything better than the Disciples' friendship with Jesus? How could you improve on their experience of knowing him, walking with him, sharing meals with him? What could be better than being able to slip through the crowds to ask him a pressing question, or to reach out for a healing touch?

What could possibly be better than having God among you?

What could be better?

Having God *within* you.

This is what Christ promised. This was the permanent source of comfort he guaranteed. This was his design to plant the voice of God inside the people of faith.

"I will ask the Father, and he will give you another Counselor, the Spirit of truth, to be with you forever. The world cannot accept this Counselor, because it neither sees him nor knows him. But you know him, for he lives with you and will be in you. I will not leave you as orphans, I will come to you. On that day you will realize that I am in my Father, and you are in me, and I am in you" (14:16–18, 20).

Christ could so boldly say, "I will not leave you comfort-less," because it was his plan to not leave us God-less.

Suppose it is true, precisely as Christ said it. We who trust God are host to God himself; his Spirit now lives within us. God speaks his mind to us, expressing his will, conveying his love. Do we experience life as we would expect it to be, if God is truly alive within us?

If God were actually speaking his mind to us, expressing his will, conveying his love, would we expect him to be so disappointingly silent and still? If God lived within us, and we knew it with certainty, wouldn't his voice rise above our confusion and doubt and pain? Wouldn't it ring with unmistakable clarity, putting the perplexity of human experience in comforting perspective?

Wouldn't his voice burn like fire through the mysteries of life? Wouldn't it shake the structure of human opinion to its foundation? Wouldn't it blast through life with hurricane force, flattening contradiction in its path?

If God lived within us, wouldn't his voice be heard dramatically above all the conflicting voices of our experience? Could we ever doubt that he lives within us, if he lives within us?

What happens when you are all alone, and heartache comes, and a hint of doubt eats at the edges of your faith, and it is just you and God?

Elijah, the prophet, experienced God in what was clearly an exception: one of the Old Testament's rare miracles. But not that many hours passed before he fell into deep depression and serious doubt. He needed comfort as only God could convey it. In an expression of encouragement for him, and I am sure for us as well, God gave a clear and memorable demonstration of his voice, there in the desert.

"A great and powerful wind tore the mountains apart and shattered the rocks before the Lord, but the Lord was not in the wind. After the wind there was an earthquake, but the Lord was not in the earthquake. After the earthquake came a fire, but the Lord was not in the fire. And after the fire came a gentle whisper" (1 Kings 19:11–12).

When Elijah heard that gentle whisper, he knew he had heard the voice of God. Could he ever forget the point? Life is boisterous; God is quiet. Present. But quiet.

Christ promised that he would not leave us comfortless. The promise is fulfilled for people of faith; they are host to God's Spirit. That same Spirit, alive within us, conveys to us the voice of God. But he most often does so in a whisper.

"Who has known the mind of the Lord
that he may instruct him?"
But we have the mind of Christ.
1 Corinthians 2:16

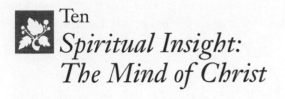

Ten

Spiritual Insight:
The Mind of Christ

What does it mean to say God speaks, but that his voice may not rise above a whisper? Or to say God is silent, but that his silence is articulate?

It means at least this: God is not indifferent to our needs or unwilling to speak. He may not say what we'd like to hear. He may not speak to certain issues that concern us. He may not shout above the distractions of life. He may not reconcile every contradiction or resolve every mystery.

We may experience silence.

But he has spoken.

There is so much more to be heard in the voice of God than most of us ever absorb. More is being transmitted than most of us are receiving.

We can preoccupy ourselves with the silence—what isn't getting through. Or we can listen for the whisper of God, learn the language of God, and wonder at those mysteries of God that have now become open secrets to those who have ears to hear.

Søren Kierkegaard, the Danish philosopher/theologian, had an uncommon way of processing thoughts and expressing ideas. His parables bristle with wit as well as insight. It seems appropriate to paraphrase him here.

A barefoot country peasant traveled to the city to earn some money. His day in the city was so profitable that he was able to buy his first pair of shoes and socks with enough money left over to get drunk. By nightfall the intoxicated peasant was understandably exhausted. When he tried to find his way home, he fell asleep in the middle of the road.

Later that night, a horse-drawn wagon came along. Seeing the drunk in the street, the driver hollered, "Get out of the way, or I'll run over your legs!" The groggy peasant awoke and looked at his legs. But since he was not accustomed to seeing shoes and socks on his feet, he did not recognize them and so called out, "Drive on, they're not my legs!"

Kierkegaard raised the question: "How can you talk about the spiritual life to someone who doesn't even realize he has a soul?"

Some of us know we have a soul, yet to some degree we are strangers to it—strangers to our own essential spiritual self. So how are we to connect with who we truly are? How are we to hear what God is already saying?

I do not think of myself as an airline evangelist, but while traveling I do occasionally find myself in conversations that matter. A few years ago, I was pulled into one such conversation before we even pushed off from the gate at Washington's Dulles International Airport. The talk turned naturally, effortlessly, to eternal matters even before that 727 lifted off the runway. It continued without interruption for a couple hours until that jet's wheels touched pavement at our destination.

Diana was a girl in her early twenties, friendly, poised. (I say "girl" rather than "woman" because of the aura of adolescence that hung about her.) Throughout our conversation, a deceptively pleasant smile was never more than a minute or two away. But Diana was separated by 1,500 miles from the twenty-one-month-old son she had out of wedlock. The baby was being cared for by her parents, and she did not get along with them well at all. The baby's father, disinterested in a pregnant girl or young mother or the responsibility of fatherhood, was gone; he said he didn't love her anymore. Diana was working long hours, trying to earn enough money to reclaim her child and raise him right, but the wait was hard. In the meantime, she drank too much and hung out with friends incapable of giving her the help she most needed.

Her search for herself and for some significance in the eyes of others had led her into the arms of one exploitative loser after another. She had turned to substance abuse to cover her sense of worthlessness. Yet floating in the back of her mind for two years was the haunting image of her folks, caring for her child.

Diana was on her way home after visiting her parents and her young son. Hopefully, before too many more months, she would be ready to return to what she knew to be her responsibility. But she was not prepared to break with the negative influences that had become her downward spiral.

For two hours we talked about God. We spoke of his love, the prospect of forgiveness and a new beginning, as well as the availability of professional counsel to help her turn good intention into lasting change. As we spoke of Christ, I could tell that it stirred something deep inside her, something out of a childhood experience, perhaps. But though she seemed to find faith intriguing, there was an obvious clash of values and ideas and allegiances within her. Change can be so difficult when life seems to shout and God seems to whisper.

I walked down the jetway and headed toward the baggage claim area preoccupied with two thoughts. I was amazed at the difference my faith had made in my life—how I had come to live and think in new patterns. I was reminded of this as I articulated my beliefs to Diana and as I compared my experience to hers. How different my own life could so easily have been. Faith had taught me ideas that were, in fact, counter to commonly accepted wisdom. And though Diana's thinking was heartbreakingly convoluted, the values that had led to her life's destructive patterns are values widely held in contemporary culture—exaggerated, perhaps, but widely held.

The other observation stuck with me for hours. It returned to the forefront of my thinking days, even weeks later. It is the reason I recall the incident with such clarity now, so many months later. Diana accepted much of the Bible as fact and stepped to the very threshold of a new perspective, yet could not cross the line. She saw that her behavior was self-destructive; she gave assent to the love and wisdom of Christ. She could not will herself to act on that information, to personalize it in faith and make it hers.

Though frustrating, this is not a novel experience. I have observed it many times. But it reminds me again how hard it is for us to break from all that would distract us, long enough to consider that we have a soul that needs our attention.

Thinking of it now, the incident also reminds me how prone I am, on some level, to do the same. We may wonder how we are to talk about spiritual things to someone who does not even know she has a soul. But we who acknowledge spiritual truth must ask ourselves why God's voice, quiet though it may be, gets so little of our attention. I say I am a person of faith, I believe God has spoken, but what am I doing with the information I have heard and need to hear?

I did not fully understand the implications when I became a Christian. I had found the freedom of forgiveness. I knew that in some sense Christ had entered my experience, my life, in the person of the Holy Spirit. I had heard and accepted those words; their implications are still only slowly settling in now, so many years later. I can scarcely comprehend the significance of it. It is mystery; but it is a mystery that has become an open secret.

When the implications of faith took hold of the apostle Paul, it tore his life inside out—quite constructively. It revolutionized his sense of purpose. God had spoken; he had revealed himself in Christ, and Paul was driven to uncover the depth of that mystery and to share it with everyone he encountered.

"My purpose," he said, "is that [people] may be encouraged in heart and united in love, so that they may have the full riches of complete understanding, in order that they may know the mystery of God, namely, Christ, in whom are hidden all the treasures of wisdom and knowledge" (Colossians 2:2–3).

Is it possible that God would turn a mystery into an open secret, and we would miss it? Could it be that the treasures of wisdom and knowledge would be revealed in Christ, but we would not dig down to uncover the full riches of complete understanding? Is it possible that God would express deep mysteries of his will, his ways, his nature, but we would only scratch the surface of comprehension? Could it be that God has spoken, but we have not heard?

Again, I paraphrase the philosopher.

❧

Imagine a sea captain who had passed every written test with flying colors, but who had not yet been to sea. How

would he react the first time he was in a storm? He knows what
the books say, but he has never tried to navigate on an overcast
night. Nor has he tried to steer a vessel when the wheel has
become a toy for the churning sea. Nor has he had to make
split-second decisions while bobbing like a cork on the mon-
strous swells. The inexperienced sea captain has no idea what
it's like to have to apply the information he has learned.

And Kierkegaard asked: "What do you do with the facts
you learn?"

Consider again Paul the Apostle, and mysteries that are
now open secrets. From prison he pens a letter to the
church at Ephesus. His friends there are concerned about
his chains, but he wants them to understand how small a
matter life's hardships can be once you know you've heard
the voice of God.

"In reading this," he tells them, "you will be able to
understand my insight into the mystery of Christ, which was
not made known to men in other generations as it has now
been revealed by the Spirit to God's holy apostles and
prophets" (Ephesians 3:4–5).

The mystery, he explains, is that God is doing something new in the world. Old boundaries like race and social
standing and gender were breaking down as God established
"one body," the church. As highly as individualism might be
valued, God was mystically at work in a unique group, the
church. As gifted as any one person might be, as full of
insight, it was God's determination that he would show himself and raise his voice as diverse people came together in
the church. There were dimensions of the will and ways and
nature of God that were to be expressed and understood not
so much in the context of individualism, as in the context of
the church together.

Paul spoke of the administration of God's mystery, "which for ages past was kept hidden in God, who created all things." And he told the Ephesian Christians, as he tells us, "[God's] intent was that now, through the church, the manifold wisdom of God should be made known to the rulers and authorities in the heavenly realms, according to his eternal purpose which he accomplished in Christ Jesus our Lord. In him and through faith in him we may approach God with freedom and confidence" (3:9–12).

It is quite difficult for us as contemporary, individualistic, Western Christians to understand the importance of the group—the community of believers—or to value the church. But imagine: after the death of Christ, people of faith had access only to the Old Testament. They had been scattered and confused. Now God's voice was raising other ideas, growing out of the fulfillment of the Old Testament Scriptures and the new things he was doing in the world. Without a completed Bible, how would those mysteries become open secrets? Individuals would gather together as the church and would learn from the apostles and the prophets, and from one another, as the Spirit of God moved mystically through them all. Only in time would this new insight be committed to the writings that would become the New Testament.

Anticipating their need, Jesus promised to send "the Spirit of truth" (John 14:17) to his disciples who would lay the foundation of the church. He told them, "The Counselor, the Holy Spirit, whom the Father will send in my name, will teach you all things and will remind you of everything I have said to you" (14:26).

"I have much more to say to you, more than you can now bear. But when he, the Spirit of truth, comes, he will guide you into all truth. He will not speak on his own; he will speak only what he hears, and he will tell you what is yet to come" (16:12–13).

Years later, still prior to the New Testament's completion, as false teaching seeped into the church, John wrote of a mysterious "anointing" from God. Because of this experience or this gift, the people of faith were taught by God himself. They did not have to be deceived and led away from the truth. They had the capacity within themselves to discern the difference between the Spirit of truth and the spirit of falsehood (1 John 2:26–27).

Paul expressed a parallel concept when he wrote: "'No eye has seen, no ear has heard, no mind has conceived what God has prepared for those who love him'—but God has revealed it to us by his Spirit." Then he voiced the rhetorical question: "Who has known the mind of the Lord that he may instruct him?" The implied answer: No one. "But," he continued, "we have the mind of Christ" (1 Corinthians 2:9–10, 16).

This is a remarkable claim.

We have heard the voice of God.

We have the mind of Christ.

And Peter wrote: "We have the word of the prophets made more certain, and you will do well to pay attention to it, as to a light shining in a dark place, until the day dawns and the morning star rises in your hearts. Above all, you must understand that no prophecy of Scripture came about by the prophet's own interpretation. For prophecy never had its origin in the will of man, but men spoke from God as they were carried along by the Holy Spirit" (2 Peter 1:19–21).

Now, is there a discrepancy between these promises of enlightenment and the amount of illumination that is ours? As we tune in and out of the conversation, God continues patiently speaking. Are we too spellbound by the distractions of life to turn our attention, undivided, to the voice of God?

I am amazed by how much energy life requires. Life is demanding, and its demands are distracting. It would be easy to exhaust a lifespan without beginning to live at all. It would be easy to waste the experience of being alive, to never even begin to think about what truly matters.

To hear the voice of God, there must be a choice. Deliberate action must be taken to shut out the distraction and focus on what matters.

"You are my friends," Christ said, "if you do what I command. I no longer call you servants, because a servant does not know his master's business. Instead, I have called you friends, for everything that I learned from my Father I have made known to you" (John 15:14–15).

As I read those words, questions crowd my mind.

By this test, can I call myself a friend of Christ? Am I doing what he commands? Am I certain I know what those commands are? Have I heard his voice? Do I care about his business? Have I made it a priority to know what that business is?

I find it remarkable that Jesus would say, "Everything I learned from my Father I made known to you." Shouldn't this spark an unquenchable curiosity? If we believed this, if we were certain that God had spoken through Christ and made his will known to us by his Spirit, would we allow anyone or anything to distract our attention from that message?

But we are distracted.

Easily and willingly.

I paraphrase the philosopher once again.

If a class of students is allowed an hour to complete an essay test and one student completes his before the time is up, he isn't penalized, is he? The assignment was to write an essay, not merely to use the time.

But what if using the time were the assignment? If a person is told to use an entire day profitably, but he becomes bored and diverted by mid-morning, wasting the balance of the day, then his speed is worthless.

The same is true when life is the task. To be finished with life before life has finished with us is to have failed to complete the assignment.

And Kierkegaard asked: "Do you ever complete the task of developing your character?"

When I think of this time-test called life, I am reminded of another mystery that has become an open secret.

"Listen, I tell you a mystery. We will not all sleep, but we will all be changed—in a flash, in the twinkling of an eye, at the last trumpet. For the trumpet will sound, the dead will be raised imperishable, and we will be changed" (1 Corinthians 15:51–52).

This time-test life, complete with its distractions, is temporary. But it is not all there is. In the final analysis, all that truly matters has been expressed in the voice of God. I cannot bear to think that I would waste my life, attentive to distraction, and not bend my concentration to every nuance of that voice.

I want a contrast in my life, a dramatic before-and-after, a spiritual turning point. It is not simply a "salvation experience" that I desire. What I am seeking is a new way of seeing, a new hierarchy of what's important, a new system to govern my thoughts and direct my feelings. I want my faith to color my perception. I want to be truly and thoroughly Christian.

For years I have preoccupied myself with the questions I have. Now I want to change all that. I want to listen for the answers God offers, even if they have nothing to do with my questions.

I have allowed myself to be distracted by life and its cares—by concerns that I may sooner or later recognize as mundane. I want my life to be consumed with the mind of God and the priorities of Christ.

I have cherished my human viewpoint and relied on our common fallible wisdom. I crave a transcendent perspective.

A fire broke out backstage in a theater on the opening night of a new comedy production. A clown realized the danger and pushed through the curtains to alert the audience.

They applauded.

The clown repeated his warning more urgently. By now he was center-stage, flailing his arms, his eyes wide in panic.

The crowd went wild. Whistles. Cheers. Raucous laughter. Never had they seen such a routine!

And I think the world will come to an end in the same way. The human race will stand in thunderous ovation, calling for an encore, convinced it's just another happy joke.

And Kierkegaard asked: "What if you try to warn the world?"

And I ask: "What if I try to warn myself?"

Let the word of Christ dwell in you richly as you teach and admonish one another with all wisdom.
Colossians 3:16

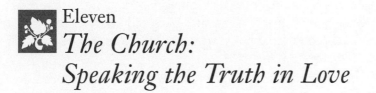 Eleven
The Church: Speaking the Truth in Love

I did not discover God on my own. His voice neither thundered from heaven nor rustled quietly in my mind. Nothing outwardly supernatural transpired.

I discovered God through people of faith. I heard his voice because others recounted his word. His mysteries became open secrets when others who knew them shared them. I learned because I was taught.

God's Spirit has introduced me to those ideas, yes. But most often others have been the conduit of spiritual insight. God, it seems, has determined that my spiritual experience and yours are to be interrelated.

But faith is more fascinatingly interdependent even than this. Faith is not only shared experience, it is legacy. I hear the voice of God today, and it is possible for me to believe because hundreds of years ago Abraham obeyed God and a nation that was to bless the nations was born. Moses responded to the voice of God and urged Hebrew families to recount divine precepts to their children and their children's children, passing on the ways of God through sacred oral tradition. Prophets spoke as God prompted them. Apostles wrote letters in response to the Spirit's nudge. Wise and faithful believers sensed what ought to be copied, distributed, shared, translated, taught. From one generation to the next, the voice of God was raised through faithful people, from house to house, from city to city, and around the world.

Schools have been founded, churches established, books written. To hear the voice of God and understand the mind of Christ is not simply a private, personal pursuit. It is the quest of the people of faith together. It is, and has been, the passion of the church.

My experiences with the church, however, have not always been so exalted. I first attended as a child because neighbors down the street were trying to plant a church in our suburban Los Angeles community. We met for Sunday school and for worship on their driveway, in their garage, in their living room, their kitchen; wherever they could find space for a few more folding chairs.

What spiritual insight did I derive from the experience? Well, I remember the perfect-attendance train. On your first Sunday, you received a colorful picture on card stock, suitable for framing, which featured train tracks prominently. Each subsequent week you were given a section of train to paste to the track. I wasn't there the week they passed out the engine and was so demotivated I did not return.

A few years later we visited a "real" church, complete with pipe organ. This experience also left an impression. I went home that Sunday afternoon and pulled out my accordion, trying to replicate the majestic organ music by punching chord buttons at random and yanking on the bellows.

It was in my third church that I began to learn what really seemed to constitute the American religious experience. I liked my Sunday school teacher. He is one of the first Christians I recall meeting, and he was everything I expected a religious person to be: kind, friendly, and interesting. I was bewildered when he quit coming to church, and stories filtered down to my naïve ears that he had been "unfaithful" and had left his wife and children for another woman.

I attended that church intermittently over the years, but it was always easier for me to find hypocrisy there than true faith, which says more about me, actually, than it does about the church. In that church, however, hypocrisy was symbolized for me by one irascible old man who talked religiously but always tried to run the church.

He would often lead singing on Sunday evenings, peppering the song time with stories of how the hymns came to be written. This confused me somewhat; I could not understand why the church would put its imprimatur on this man, who was so often criticized for his snarling temperament.

He stepped to the podium one Sunday evening, announced the hymn, "Amazing Grace," and before the pianist could stumble through an intro, he said, "Have I ever told you the story of how this great hymn came to be written?"

A diminutive elderly woman interrupted, her voice edged with exasperation. "Yes," she said, speaking for us all, "many times."

This church may not have been fertile soil for the seed of faith to grow, but God seems to delight in achieving the unexpected through unlikely means. It was in this church that I became a Christian, memorized the great hymns of faith, learned what it means to serve Christ, discovered that the Bible did not have to be boring, and decided I would serve God with my life.

What made the difference? Three or four faithful people who treated me in kindness, as I imagined Christ would treat me. It was their lives that made me curious about their words, and those words turned out to be not theirs alone, but his.

In this church, through mere humans like me, with obvious foibles, I heard the voice of God.

I was in college when I became involved in ministry elsewhere and, therefore, changed my church affiliation. This new church, the whole denomination as it turned out, placed quite a premium on the details of Bible study. By my judgment, those details were not always accurately interpreted.

I sat through a new members class amazed, as a well-meaning gentleman who knew nothing of Greek made the Greek New Testament say remarkable things—what you might call highly debatable nuances of meaning. When I took my first Greek class, the prof wisely warned us: "There's nothing more dangerous in the pulpit than a first-year Greek student." My experience suggests that the danger only gradually diminishes with the subsequent few years.

I do not wish to sound overly critical. I deeply appreciate the zeal this church and its denomination has for the Scriptures. But each denomination's doctrinal distinctives and private interpretations so easily take on weight equal to the Bible itself.

This church had a motto, which, though I value the sentiment, always reminded me of a television courtroom melodrama: "The Bible, the whole Bible, and nothing but the Bible." As a seminary student, working for the denomination's Christian education department, I was responsible for preparing instructional materials for a series on the denomination's heritage and distinctives. For an introductory unit, I created two posters. One featured the motto mentioned above. The other captured what I understood to be a logical extension of it, and the passion, I thought, of the church. It read: "The Bible—primary. The church's historical position—secondary."

One angry pastor who received the materials fired back a letter expressing bewilderment that such a distinction would be drawn. "If I did not think our historical position was biblical, I would not be a member of this church!"

This, I believe, graphically portrays the problem of the church and the danger that is implicit with the voice of God being entrusted to us fallible, finite humans. I have said that I discovered God through people of faith. I have known many who shun God for the same reason. They find our array of conflicting beliefs perplexing. They find our intolerance of divergent viewpoints distasteful. It is bad enough that we disagree; must we also be disagreeable?

At that time, I found myself shifting my own categories. Where once I perceived interpretations or doctrinal positions as being either biblical or unbiblical, I now toyed with a third category: more biblical than the Bible. Was it possible that in our zeal to understand the Scripture—and to defend its truth against error—that we would elevate our own interpretive schemes to the point that they would overshadow the truth we sought to explain? Could our denominational distinctives and traditions take on authority properly reserved for Scripture alone?

The Bible did not seem to me to put forth every teaching with equal clarity. Weren't there subtleties in Scripture that faithful and knowledgeable people interpreted differently? How far should our drive for biblical understanding carry us?

It seems to me that it is possible for logic to lead us further than do the clear statements of Scripture. When the logic of our theological systems begins to fill in the gaps left by Scripture's mysteries and incongruities, we are on precarious ground.

And there are incongruities and mysteries.

Which should come as no surprise.

Scripture has forewarned us that as we seek the mind of God, we will encounter the limits of our own thinking.

"My thoughts are not your thoughts,
  neither are your ways my ways," declares the Lord.
"As the heavens are higher than the earth,

so are my ways higher than your ways
and my thoughts than your thoughts." (Isaiah 55:8–9)

Oh, the depth of the riches of the wisdom and knowledge of God!
How unsearchable his judgments,
and his paths beyond tracing out!
"Who has known the mind of the Lord?
Or who has been his counselor?" (Romans 11:33–34)

I would not want to try to understand God apart from the wisdom of the church, but neither would I want to let any humanly devised theological system dictate clarity for Scripture where clarity seems deliberately to be lacking. When at last I have God figured out, and when I withdraw into my own system or movement, looking suspiciously on all others in the family of faith, I am most certainly in error.

God is bigger than my theology, his family more inclusive than my movement.

Yet isn't it odd that it would even be possible for people of faith to differ and fracture into diverse movements? If God intended to entrust his truth to the church, why would he permit any hint of ambiguity, any alternate shade of meaning?

To myself, at this moment as I write, I say the words "the silence of God," and what comes to my mind? Mystery. For not all of life's mysteries have become open secrets. I may find God silent when I face pain and perplexity. In my hurt, it is unlikely that I will receive my own private word from God, explaining the particulars of my negative or challenging experience. I hurt, and my pain is met with silence.

But for me, the silence of God has another dimension. God speaks, yet his very expressions of truth may feel at times ambiguous. Since we find such dissonance distasteful, we frame as many viewpoints as we have denominations. A plethora of opinion. With so many contradictory voices speaking for God, without him supernaturally correcting the misconceptions, we may have a hard time calling the resulting cacophony, "the voice of God."

God has spoken. The church has relayed the message. But in the static of our divergent, human interpretations, what so often is heard instead of the voice of God is his silence.

It does seem odd that God would entrust his voice, his truth, to something as fragile as the church. Certainly, God knew that in doing so he was opening himself to misunderstanding and misrepresentation. Why would he do it?

I am perplexed.

It is, though, consistent with the nature of God to risk everything on fragile containers. After all, God himself appeared in the weakness of a human body, so easily broken and destroyed. And yet, its glory was its brokenness, for out of brokenness the power of God was displayed.

Is it really any different with the church?

Nearly two thousand years have come and gone. The voice of God has at times been twisted into the most bizarre ideologies. Movements have risen and fallen. Opinion and personal conflict have splintered the people of faith. But such opinion and misrepresentation cannot suppress the voice of God for long. The Spirit is alive in the church, granting perception to those who have ears to hear with humility.

With all our diversity and misunderstanding, it may seem to be a miracle that anyone believes.

But isn't that, precisely, the point?

Doesn't God seem to delight in achieving the unexpected through unlikely means?

"God opposes the proud, but gives grace to the humble."
. . . Come near to God and he will come near to you.
James 4:6, 8

 Twelve
Perspective:
Teaching the Silence to Talk

A man once found a key while walking along the beach at dusk. He picked it up and turned it over in his hands. Immediately, he recognized that it had been forged from solid gold and inlaid with precious stones. He imagined it had great significance and value.

Even so, he said to himself, it serves no useful purpose. What could it possibly open here, on this deserted beach?

Again he turned the key in his palm, toying with the setting sun as it reflected on the precious stones. Then, noting that the sun was low on the horizon and night was fast approaching, the man pitched the key into the waves and turned to hurry off. What he failed to notice was that before him stood a massive doorway in the darkening sky.

There is another world, a parallel reality, a spiritual realm beyond the reach of our limited physical senses. For most of us, perhaps all of us, there is a critical moment when those spiritual realities are close. A hand stretched out in faith could take the key, treasure it, fit it into the lock, turn the latch, and open the door. At that crisis point of decision or awareness, faith would carry us over the threshold, if only we would allow it.

At this turning point, some look forward into that other realm, and the spiritual reality they see suddenly appears to be all that truly matters in life. Standing at that doorway, they look in and see life for what it can be. How could anything that had gone before hold value now, compared to this? At this same decisive juncture, others, in denial, look away, because they are only capable of seeing life as they imagine that it is or has been. They trust their physical senses alone and so turn away, their backs to all that will someday matter.

I used to think there was this one critical, life-changing moment only, when we either embraced spiritual reality or turned away from it. I now see that all of our moments offer such crucial choice, such perspective-altering potential. Spiritual reality calls me to live every experience, each moment, with the heavens in view. To make every decision in faith, governed by the unseen. To see every chance encounter as a holy moment. To face the mystery of pain, and find somewhere traces of the compassion and purpose of God. To confront the contradictions and incongruities that perplex my limited mind, and humbly trust God's greater wisdom. To create stillness amid the distractions of life and to will myself to hear the voice of God.

To do this is to live.

But where does such perception come from?

Once in a faraway land with a strange culture and different language, a man was offered a gift. The host pulled a small book from a shelf and extended it to the visitor without speaking. Such was the custom in his land. Gifts were offered without fanfare and without compulsion.

But the visitor stood, merely staring at his host, disgusted that his culture and ways were so peculiar. Besides, he could not read a foreign book. He glared at his host's face, whose eyes betrayed sadness. This also irked the stranger. So typically melodramatic, he thought.

Still the host stood, sorrowful, but patient, extending the gift. Finally, the stranger nodded awkwardly, excused himself, and departed. The host, offended though not surprised, left the house and walked out into the city streets, still holding the rejected gift.

Soon he encountered another stranger to whom he offered the gift in the same fashion. The second stranger accepted the gift with a gesture of appreciation. When he opened the book, he discovered that it was handwritten in the unknown language of the host.

Curiously, as the stranger examined the book, he received a second, mysterious gift: the ability to read with comprehension. As he did so, he recognized that the book contained fascinating secrets of life—the answers to his unexpressed questions.

❦

It would be easy to dismiss the story as trite fantasy. Except some of us have experienced this; we have received the gift. We have passed it on to others. We have watched as spiritual gibberish dissolved into profound meaning. We have been changed by words and have witnessed the transformation of others by them.

God's voice may be unheard, but he has spoken. And the words, heard in faith, will not leave us as once we were.

I have written of my experience with God's Book, affirming its transforming properties. I read mere words and find I am hearing the voice of God. I obey the Book, and I more fully apprehend its meaning. To some extent, at least, I have slogged through the history, culture, geography, and languages of the Bible. As my understanding of these critical contexts has deepened, so has my grasp of biblical principles. In Scripture, I hear the voice of God. In Scripture, I gaze, at times mesmerized, at the portrait of his character —his work, his will, his ways—painted in the experience of individuals and nations. In Scripture, through faith, I find my life transformed, my perspective changed, my mind renewed.

The host has offered a foreign gift, a revelation of himself and all that matters, in a book he himself has authored. I have accepted the gift, I have examined the book, and slowly its meaning is opening to me.

Were I to stop here, however, I would give too limiting an interpretation of the gift, and a somewhat dishonest representation of my own spiritual pilgrimage. For though I hear the voice of God in Scripture, profound and rich, and though it is the point of reference and judge of all of my spiritual experiences, yet there is more to be said of both God's self-disclosure and his persistent silence.

God speaks. Certainly, God speaks. But not as I converse with you or you with me. His voice is, it seems, more frustratingly indirect.

Israel cried out for a king. Why? Because unlike a human earthly king, God was invisible and silent.

In asserting the existence of God, Scripture appeals to Creation and to the faithfulness of God—what he has made and what he has done. Why? Because God himself is unseen and unheard. If we would "see" him, we must look at what he has done.

God calls on people to speak for him; he does not generally spread his word through direct encounters as he once did with Paul. Why? Because God is invisible and silent.

Certainly, he spoke with Moses, "face to face, as a friend speaks to a friend"; he walked with Enoch; he revealed himself to prophets in dreams, visions, and supernatural appearances. But these were the exceptions, not his customary manner of communicating with people. We see in Christ the supreme revelation of God, because finally God fully disclosed himself—the Word became flesh—yet he returned to heaven, hiding himself from our view. He sent the Spirit to live within us and to illuminate his Word, yet when I pray, I receive no audible response.

When I am heartbroken over the mystery of pain, no divine voice scatters the silence with reassuring words. When I crave the companionship of God, I do not meet him through my five physical senses. Scripture offers principles, it illustrates the purpose and character of God, but to truly hear that voice in my experience, another step must be taken. I must teach the silence to talk. Or more to the point, I must teach myself to hear God's voice in the silence.

I must lift the key and open the door.

I must take the gift, open it, and read.

I must learn to live, as Paul expresses it, "by faith, not by sight" (2 Corinthians 5:7).

By putting faith and sight in contradistinction, Scripture is not saying that God is unapproachable, that he cannot be perceived or known. He can be "seen," just not in the customary manner. He can be "heard," but not just with our ears. He can be "felt," but not with these human hands. Alongside our physical senses, there must be a spiritual conduit of sensation. A different sense. Another avenue of truth.

Faith.

"Without faith it is impossible to please God, because anyone who comes to him must believe that he exists and that he rewards those who earnestly seek him" (Hebrews 11:6).

What does it mean to earnestly seek him, in faith? Among other things, it means to nurture the perspective of

God alive and active in life's every moment. If God chooses the invisible, as he has, I will live by faith. If God chooses silence, I will create quiet so that he may be heard. I will contemplate what sense denies me. I will fill my heart with what will not fill my vision. I will fill my mind with what will not fill my ears. I will give my imagination a theological education.

I will visualize God as near to me. I will feel his arms holding me. Hear his voice encouraging me. This is not as far-fetched as it may at first seem.

Think of the conception of Jesus. In the womb of the Virgin Mary, in that microscopic beginning, not only was there all the essence there would ever be of the man Jesus, there was also all there was of God. Undiminished deity in a speck of space.

Similarly, through the promise of the Spirit, all that there is of God is living within us. We often think of the immensity of God. He fills all the universe. But also, all that there is of God is concentrated within me. It is impossible to get more of God. He is not parceled up and distributed around the infinite stretch of space. He is here, all of him, within me. In all his limitless power. In all his incomprehensible wisdom. In all his loving kindness.

This is truly astounding: This God is willing to call me his home!

For a moment, put aside all you have ever heard or known of faith, and ask yourself: What would it be like if through some miracle, God could live within me? How would life be different? Certainly, it would change everything.

So why hasn't it? Why isn't life as consistently dramatic as you'd expect? And where is the voice of God? How can life feel so ordinary while God is at home inside us?

Or is it possible that "the ordinary" is the point?

Could it be that God intends to fill the ordinary with new meaning? Is it conceivable that God is present and speaking through every experience and that through faith we may see his face and hear his voice? Is this what it means to teach the silence to talk?

Last night as I sat with my wife at the kitchen table, I looked into her eyes as concern crossed her face. Lately, we have been dealing with some challenging circumstances. The particulars do not matter at this point. As I looked at her, I felt compassion. And I loved her. Twenty minutes later, we sat together in the living room as I read aloud an amusing short story by the British humorist P. G. Wodehouse. My wife's laughter was music. And I loved her. The private evening together ended upstairs, in intimacy. And I loved her.

Last night's diversity is emblematic of our marriage. There have been times of considerable hardship and tears; there has been the celebration of joy and laughter; there has been romance. Today, as I reflect on our relationship, this gift, I am struck by the presence of God throughout our union. He is present in our relationship not just when we are reading something religious, not just when we are involved in ministry together, not just when we are focused on his grace and overcome with worship. God is present in the mundane also, in every moment. He is speaking, if we will hear it—speaking of his kindness, his faithfulness, his sovereign lordship over circumstance, his mercy in heartache, his mirth in our success. The gift of this relationship is not merely an illustration of God's faithfulness or grace, he speaks through the gift because he is alive within it.

I am thinking of a man who pastored my small church many years ago. From a supply of many excellent memories I select one. We were standing together in the darkened church parking lot, having just completed an evening Bible study. The few in attendance had departed. Out of the quiet, this pastor, my friend, told me, "One person who truly believed, could turn this city upside down." As he said this, it did not sound silly or sensational; it sounded only truthful. And I realized I wanted to be that one believing person. In that encounter so many years ago, I heard two voices, for God was alive in our friendship on a dark night in Whittier, California, almost thirty years ago.

Next week I will go to court with a different friend. I will convey my love and my support, even though he is guilty of a criminal offense. Today as I write, I do not know what the outcome will be. But as I have observed him, I can see the consequences of his repeated inappropriate actions slowly closing in around him. And I am certain that God is speaking to him through those consequences, through the reproofs of life itself. His experiences not only confirm the counsel of Scripture; God's voice can be heard in those experiences, if he will find the grace to listen without defensiveness.

I spent yesterday afternoon at a museum, awed by the work of a contemporary artist. His use of scale and dimension, texture, and light astounded me. His eye for detail, the perfection of his rendering, commanded my attention. I felt a hush, a holiness, in the presence of such art, and I worshipped the Giver. I have had parallel experiences listening to great music, reading fine literature, watching an exceptional film. Can you understand me if I say God's voice can be heard through the gift of art, that it echoes his own creativity, that it illuminates the world he has made? As imperfect as our creations may be, aren't there times when you are certain that God has willingly visited them with his own voice?

I watched as a shooting star streaked the night sky. I marveled at a dolphin's graceful arc. I wondered at the slow but certain growth of a giant redwood.

The Creation is not simply a completed work of art, hanging, framed in the universe, merely representing the characteristics of our God. In observing nature, we are looking over the shoulder of the Artist, still active in the creative process. As each moment brings a new and astounding brushstroke, God speaks. To tune into nature with such biblical perspective is not to flirt with New Age nonsense; it is to pay attention to the voice of God, speaking through all he has made and is making, through all he sustains by his powerful word.

To express all this yet one other way: Though the Bible is the interpreter and judge of all my spiritual experiences, it is not God's sole voice. His words are not conveyed through Scripture alone. He has many ways of speaking. Nature is his mouthpiece, and relationships and circumstances. Success and failure, joy and sorrow, art and science, star and atom, the wilderness and the wind.

When our understanding is filled with his works; when our mind perceives his way; when our heart worships the mysteries of his person; when we see his sovereign hand controlling epochs and milliseconds; then his voice can be heard in everything.

Even in his silence.

And this is the key I hold and treasure.

Part Three
The Mystery of God
It is the nature of faith
to live with paradox.

*About many of our questions
there remains a maddening
open-endedness.
How are we to reconcile
faith's conflicting ideas and
life's dissonant experiences?*

The Lord is not slow in keeping his promise,
as some understand slowness.
He is patient.
2 Peter 3:9

Do not throw away your confidence. . . . In just a very
little while, "He who is coming will come and will not
delay. But my righteous one will live by faith."
Hebrews 10:35, 37

Thirteen
Partial Answers:
Living with Dissonance

When I was a seminary student in the rural Midwest, my wife and I rented the main floor, and a young single guy the basement apartment, of a house that had once been merely a summer cottage. If you read into that statement "thin walls" and "high noise transmission," you have caught my drift precisely. Because we knew that we could sit in our living room on our threadbare sofa and listen to the conversations of our downstairs neighbor and his girlfriend, we quickly learned to hold down our own volume and to plan noisier activities, like playing the stereo or practicing the piano, for times when the guy downstairs was out. This was not hard to do, since you could easily hear him leaving.

Or so I thought.

I was sure he and his girlfriend had left one bracing late October evening when I decided to take a break from parsing Greek verbs, studying Hebrew vowels, and considering the peculiarities of supralapsarianism. I stepped over to the stereo, put on a recording of Bach's "Toccata and Fugue in D Minor," cranked the volume to that point just before the speakers would self-destruct, and settled down for about nine minutes and ten seconds of full-throttle pipe-organ music. The walls shook, the windows rattled, my rib cage vibrated, and I felt a week's worth of tension leaving my weary body and overtaxed brain.

For nine minutes that amazing piece of music moved relentlessly toward its climax. It was in that brief silent break, just before those final dissonant measures resolved into a plaster-peeling D minor, that I heard the slam of the downstairs door. My quick, nervous glance out the window confirmed my apprehension: the neighbor and his girlfriend were just *leaving*, not arriving.

That week's worth of tension that had vanished moments before now returned in a rush as I dashed out the front door to apologize.

My neighbor regained his social graces in time to say, almost convincingly I think, "No problem." But his girlfriend, still frazzled, could only stammer, somewhat less reassuringly, "I thought we were in the middle of a Vincent Price horror movie!" I could not tell if I was supposed to laugh or offer my condolences. Compromising, I smiled weakly.

I have heard preachers liken this present, perplexing age to the organ's dissonant chord, aching to be resolved at time's conclusion and eternity's dawn. Well, when I run that sermon illustration through imagination's mechanism, I cross-reference it with a true life context. But in my enlightened imagination, the dissonant chord, aching to be resolved, that tests the nerves and stands the hair on end, is heard from two perspectives: mine and the neighbor's. And because there are two perspectives, there are two opinions of the music—for what relieves tension in one person may create tension in another.

I am certain that eternity's surprises will bear this out. To those unfamiliar with life's Composer, the music may seem an eerie, unsettling cacophony. Others, who know the Composer and respect his work, probably have some idea where the theme is headed, despite the twists and turns it may take in getting there.

And then the dissonant chord sermon illustration takes on a different perspective for me because it is forever locked in an amusing context. I can still see the girlfriend's bewildered look. That dimension of comedy makes the illustration all the more poignant.

I do not mean to trivialize pain and hardship, but I am convinced that when God finally completes the composition and the sounds of eternity drown out the discordant din of time, we will not all stand around long-faced and somber, bewildered and crazed. Some may, but not all of us. I can imagine the collective grin, spreading across the sea of relieved faces. I also suspect there will be, in retrospect, the silent, reflective nod of the head in recognition of the purpose of God in some of the mysteries in this life—as much as to say, "Oh, that's what the music meant."

The problem, of course, is that we're not there yet. The climax and resolution are who knows how far ahead of us. For now we live in the incomplete, which can be unnervingly dissonant. Routinely, things happen that are so distasteful that it defies the imagination to contemplate any good by-product or purpose. Any chance of lighthearted amusement may seem at times remote; just as I did not laugh about the Vincent Price allusion until later, after I had extricated myself from the embarrassing context.

It is one thing to say God now speaks to us in the ordinary, to say that his silence is articulate because in some mysterious way he is speaking through that silence. It is quite another thing to hear God's voice in confusion, paradox, and mystery—in life's discordant experiences. Even to claim, as I do, that God's character is revealed in Scripture may not feel fully satisfying when in the crucible of crisis. And for most of us, perhaps all of us, sooner or later there does come a gap in our parade of good times. Life gets hard. Our beliefs are tested. God's voice grows faint. And our faith faces its greatest challenge: partial answers and irreconcilable ideas.

In that dissonance, when everything within us clamors for complete explanations, how can a faith founded on partial answers sustain us?

I was in college when Alvin Toffler's book *Future Shock* was released. It became the topic of discussion in my psychology class as our Christian prof posed the question: "How can a responsible Christian cope with future shock?" I remember that class session now, so many years later, because I at first found his answer somewhat shocking: "Reduce your primary beliefs to a minimum," he said. "Don't hold every viewpoint and interpretation with equal tenacity."

He wasn't saying, "Empty your faith of its significance." He was saying, if I may paraphrase him: "The paramount, cornerstone truths of your faith matter. Cling to them. They will give you stability. But not every opinion merits dogmatic adherence, and there may be no way to wrap every experience in a neat package of comfortable explanations. Live long enough and you will encounter inexplicable mystery."

I can only say, "I have." And I have concluded it is easier to cope if you're willing to wait for complete answers and can tolerate a little dissonance in the meantime; though the meantime seems long and slow.

Toffler's point, I suppose, was that as change accelerates and the future invades the present, life becomes both more stressful and more challenging. How are we to cope with all that dizzying change?

But isn't there also a "present shock"? The stressful and discouraging realization that the good changes promised by God's future agenda are as yet out of reach. We must live in the present, with its hardship and confusion—its dissonance—when everything within us longs for better times or healing or justice or, at least, satisfying answers.

Resolution.

Yesterday my mother picked up the telephone and closed the 2,000-mile gap that separates us. She's called several times in the past week, and I know what's on her mind. We are approaching the first anniversary of my father's death, and though she loves God and is staking everything —her very life and her emotional equilibrium—on God's trustworthiness, this is a dark and perplexing time. How can you make sense of it?

In the same call, she gave medical updates on three of my uncles, and the reports were not uplifting. What was so clear to me, perhaps more so than to her, was that their misfortune was resonating with her memory of Dad's misfortune twelve months ago.

There she sat, fighting back tears, because she sits face-to-face with "present shock." Things now are not as they will be and, she would insist, should be. And yet, even in her darkness, light breaks through, because she is not truly locked in the present. She has already seen the future in the face of Christ, and the image is so vivid it will carry her through her confusion and sorrow. By faith she has already heard hints of life's finale. To live through its "uncertainty" now is to rehearse oddly familiar music, as if she'd heard it before in a wonderful, comforting dream. For this future vision to invade the dissonant present is not shock, it is serenity. The more certain you are of coming relief, the easier it is to endure present pain.

Dissonance. Confusion. Paradox. Mystery. Incongruity. In the painful present, we may experience tension between our expectations of God and his performance. Our glowing image of abundant life may turn dark and confusing as we enter the shadow of uncertainty, sickness, or even death. We may search the Scriptures for perspective and find that even God seems at times to contradict himself. Our carefully crafted efforts at harmonizing the dissonant ideas may not quite do the trick.

Faith can be frustrating.

No, *life* can be frustrating. Understanding can be elusive. Well-placed faith is what gives perspective and releases hope.

These mysteries matter to me, but because I have encountered God, I am willing to live with partial answers. I may struggle to find a place of comfort in the midst of incongruity, but I am giving myself permission to be human with all the limitations that implies and to let God be God with all the limitlessness that implies. If I am certain of God, life's every detail needn't make sense within the cramped perspective of my own puny understanding, frail intellectualizing, and frantic efforts at reconciling the irreconcilable. The partial answers God reveals are better than the complete explanations I might improvise. Life is God's masterwork, after all, not mine. I have no choice but to wait for his timing, as he moves it purposefully toward climax and resolution.

Even so, it is fair and appropriate to ask: What are we to do in the meantime? How are we to live in the present, with hardship so loud and dissonant and God so still and silent?

This third and concluding section of the book relates God's silence to his will and his kingdom; to faith and doubt; to prayer and divine companionship. I have approached this tapestry of ideas from several angles, even so, those common threads of thought emerge intertwined. If I am to make sense of the silence of God, I must understand his kingdom in its two tenses, present and future; I must rise above my doubt and live by my faith; I must crack the code of prayer and rest in its quiet.

There is some darkness to the next few chapters, sort of like entering a cave—or a tomb. Yet there is hope. In the darkest of circumstance, the deepest cave, the coldest tomb, something stirs, light reaches, a voice is heard.

Life happens!

It is my prayer, even now as I write, that in the end, our faith may be deeper, our hope more profoundly felt, because we have honestly faced our own limitations, yet have found reassuring perspective in the articulate silence of God.

Answer me when I call to you,
  O my righteous God.
Give me relief from my distress;
  be merciful to me and hear my prayer.
Psalm 4:1

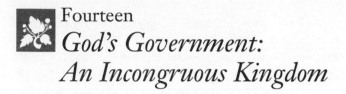 Fourteen
God's Government:
An Incongruous Kingdom

"I prayed so many times, and so hard, so hard I prayed, and nothing happened. And now I'm not so sure ... that there is a God."

With these words, freed hostage Thomas Sutherland summed up his six-and-a-half years of captivity in Lebanon. He recounted his unending ordeal, chained to the wall in a dark underground cell. He spoke in chilling terms of the day he was so badly beaten that he screamed in pain, and he told the press that he and fellow hostage Terry Anderson, both in chains, passed the time by debating religion. Sutherland took the agnostic view; Anderson argued that God does indeed exist.

After hearing his experience, you'd think that agnostic Sutherland had the distinct advantage. Isn't his viewpoint painfully understandable? After all, if God exists, if the universe is his, how can such anarchy rule? How could he let the prayers of the hostage go unanswered for more than six years?

117

Sutherland said that he pitied his captors, because "they do not appreciate how heinous the thing is that they are doing." But all around the globe such things happen and not just in the arena of political differences. Irrational, disgruntled workers take up arms and turn to rage to gain a hearing or to release their pent-up frustration. In the process, the innocent, or at least the defenseless, become the victims. Consider the world's rules of order: The weak suffer; the gentle are disregarded; the poor, the hungry, the homeless are forgotten. Almost twenty percent of the planet's 5.4 billion people live in absolute poverty and distress. Christian faith must make sense even for them if it is to make sense at all.

Suppose Christ himself were called on to explain the government of his kingdom; how would he account for such incongruity: the reign of God and the simultaneous reign of evil? If we live in the context of such terrifying possibilities, how are we to understand the authority of Christ? What can he possibly say to us that would dispel our strong suspicion that everything is out of control?

And in this world, as subjects of the unseen, silent king, how are we to live?

Jesus understood the incongruities of his kingdom. He knew who he was: both the Son of God and the child of human poverty. He knew the innuendo surrounding his birth, how his expectant parents had been ridiculed by judgmental neighbors. He also knew that the good news of his birth had meant death to Bethlehem's infant sons. He knew what it was to be misunderstood by those closest to him. He knew the oppression of life in occupied territories under often-inequitable rule. He knew, as he faced the great temptation, that the kingdoms of the world were, in some mysterious sense, Satan's possessions to offer. He knew that the land was filled with the sick to be healed, the demon-controlled to be delivered, the captives to be freed. He knew he would face betrayal and excruciating execution. He knew that we who follow him would also fail him.

He was not naïve.

He knew.

What sort of kingdom is his, then, that his world and ours should remain so frustratingly unchanged?

Of course, the people followed him at first because they suspected he *would* change the world. They faced disease and saw him as their healer. They grew hungry and clamored for him to be their provider. They languished under Rome and wondered if he might not be their liberator.

The crowds were his. Until he withheld his miracles. Until he dismissed political solutions. Until he told them to count the cost.

What sense was there in joining this no-change kingdom?

And yet, how could they—or we—misunderstand his agenda for change? All the clues were there—for them and now for us—at the beginning of his career, in the first ninety-six words of his first great sermon. We have come to call that sermon introduction, "The Beatitudes." Those ninety-six words form a sort of preamble to the Constitution of the Kingdom, the Sermon on the Mount.

Time yourself. Say them aloud, slowly, thoughtfully. The essence of the kingdom is conveyed in less than sixty seconds.

Blessed are the poor in spirit,
for theirs is the kingdom of heaven.
Blessed are those who mourn,
for they will be comforted.
Blessed are the meek,
for they will inherit the earth.
Blessed are those who hunger and thirst for righteousness,
for they will be filled.
Blessed are the merciful,
for they will be shown mercy.
Blessed are the pure in heart,
for they will see God.

Blessed are the peacemakers,
   for they will be called sons of God.
Blessed are those who are persecuted because of righteousness,
   for theirs is the kingdom of heaven. (Matthew 5:3–10)

Welcome to the invisible kingdom. The kingdom in two tenses—present and future—where what God does now, within us, foreshadows what he will do for us someday, out in the open, for all to see. In this kingdom, the ruler's subjects will thrive, though they have faced persecution. Meekness will be rewarded, sorrow taken away, legitimate desires fulfilled. Those who know how, see the face of God. Peacemakers, not warmongers, are given the place of honor. The humble, not the proud, are exalted. And in this kingdom, today and until the King returns, we undergo astonishing inward change so that we are equipped to live in a world that, for now, stubbornly refuses to change.

"Blessed."

Such an odd way to begin a sermon, and a career.

"Blessed."

"Blessed."

"Blessed."

Eight pronouncements, delineating a joy that can coexist with pain.

A deep happiness can be ours in the midst of poverty, in the face of sorrow, in the position of weakness. We value righteousness and are rewarded. We show mercy and receive it in return. We live in purity and meet the Purifier. We spread peace and are known by God's name. And if life's worst befalls us, even then the King himself is with us, his kingdom belongs to us.

I used to stumble over the Beatitudes as I read. I saw them as beautiful, religious-sounding statements. It was fitting that they should be immortalized on wall-hangings and greeting cards. But what did they mean? It was after I began considering their opposites that I felt their life-changing force.

I am blessed if I am "poor in spirit," not if I am overcome with pride over my own importance and spiritual achievements.

I am blessed if I "mourn," not if I am callous and insensitive to the pain around me.

I am blessed if I am "meek," not if I am swallowed up with greed and anger.

I am blessed if I "hunger and thirst after righteousness," not if I am indifferent toward God and his ways.

I am blessed if I am "merciful," not if I am bitter, resentful, and cold.

I am blessed if I am "pure in heart," not if my thoughts are filled with impurity.

I am blessed if I am a "peacemaker," not if I am critical, judgmental, and hostile.

I am blessed if I am "persecuted because of righteousness," not if I am ashamed of God or embarrassed to be known as his follower.

Reeling from the impact of the Beatitudes, I understood a bit more clearly why this great sermon began with those ninety-six words. The sermon's standards are impossibly high. In this kingdom, the laws are written on hearts—love your enemies, control your lust, tame your anger, withhold judgment. Who can fulfill the expectations? Only spiritually renovated people. "Blessed" people. Until I grasp these spiritual qualities, the Beatitudes, it will be so hard to even *hear* the rest of Christ's "sermon"—or any of God's conversations in Christ. That preamble puts the Constitution of the Kingdom in perspective.

But in reading these characteristics as spiritual qualities, I must not forget their earthly tone or I will miss much of what Jesus was trying to convey. That is, he used the language of poverty, sorrow, and human conflict for a reason.

Perhaps you have noticed: though the Beatitudes are recorded by both Matthew (chapter 5) and Luke (chapter 6), we tend to favor Matthew in our reading. His rendition sounds so spiritual. Luke's is more earthly. Also, as Luke relates it, Jesus speaks to us directly, in the second person.

Matthew says, "Blessed are the poor in spirit." Luke says simply, "Blessed are you who are poor."

Matthew says, "Blessed are those who hunger and thirst for righteousness." Luke says, "Blessed are you who hunger now."

Throughout Scripture, the poor, the hungry, the disenfranchised are depicted as somehow closer to the kingdom. They are less likely to trust in their own position or merit, more apt to be driven to God out of their hopelessness. Wealth, comfort, and position can so easily blind us to what matters. The discomfort of poverty, on the other hand, may open our spiritual eyes to see ourselves as we truly are.

Is it possible that lacking food would lead us to a place where we are more likely to hunger and thirst after righteousness? Could it be that our material poverty would help us to understand what it means to be poor in spirit?

It is certainly understandable that six-and-a-half years of captivity and "unanswered prayers" would lead a man to question the existence of God. But is it really surprising that another man, going through the same experience would come to a different conclusion? Couldn't such an experience drive us *to* God, if only we could make sense of his silence?

What if hardship—poverty, hunger, sorrow, even persecution—did open our eyes to see earth's invisible king, opened our ears to hear him? What if seeing him, and hearing his voice, changed us, even if our circumstances remained unchanged? Wouldn't we also find ourselves filled with a deep joy, a mysterious happiness? If we could sense God with us, even in our most severe heartache—if it is possible—wouldn't we then discover what it truly means to be "blessed"?

Is it such incongruity that drives Jesus to begin his sermon, and in a sense his career, with sixty seconds of perspective?

"Blessed."

"Blessed."

"Blessed."

We must not lightly dismiss Thomas Sutherland's 2,347 days of captivity. Neither do nice words take away the blinding sting of grief for families in this country who have lost someone they love to mindless violence or unchecked disease. The poor may not be lifted from their poverty. The hungry may remain unfed. The homeless may still search for shelter. The heart-broken may yet have reason for sorrow.

God may still be silent.

The invisible King knew we would long for justice and for some reasonable comfort. Not surprisingly, then, in this same great sermon he taught us to pray, "Your kingdom come. Your will be done on earth as it is in heaven." The outward changes we all crave will come. We will experience firsthand the kingdom's future tense.

Until then, those who know the King, who are being changed from the inside out, may discover a deep happiness, rising above circumstance. In this present tense of the kingdom, that is the great surprise. The King is alive, writing his preamble within us, and teaching us to live it:

"Blessed."

"Blessed."

"Blessed."

Your kingdom come,
your will be done on earth
*   as it is in heaven.*
Matthew 6:10

Fifteen
God's Will:
The Paradox of Power

I expected the courtroom to be larger. And warmer. Instead, this small room with its drab, off-white walls and linoleum floors confined me. Law books, filled with jargon and objectivity, lined the shelves on the west wall, while fifteen gray metal folding chairs stood in crooked rows, facing a wide table—the bench. The December cold, seeping through poorly sealed windows, added to the distance one person felt from another.

Here, this morning, the final act of a two-year trauma would be played out. Action initiated those many months earlier would terminate in one man's decision. As the morning would bring an end—to uncertainty, at least—it would also bring a beginning, of one sort or another. Here, this morning, prayer would be answered.

In truth, prayer was the point. Not one man's decision —even one man with the State behind him. God's will, I anticipated with confidence, would be done. But in the face of the silence of God, how could I presume to know what that would mean?

When my wife and I opened our home to a twenty-two-month-old ward of the court, the understanding was that he —and his younger sister, placed in another foster home— would soon be legally free for adoption. But a new state law, deemed retroactive and, therefore, applicable to this case, turned a few weeks' wait into a two-year emotional roller-coaster of uncertainty and apprehension.

And we knew too much. Even small towns have bureaucracy, but it is small-town bureaucracy. While the gears ground slowly, we were privy to details of our foster son's background that raised significant anxiety. Details we probably should not have known. If he and his sister were returned to that home, would they be safe? Would they be fed? Would they be clothed?

Would they be loved?

We prayed. Our friends prayed. But the apprehensions did not evaporate. We could ask that God's will would be done—we could ask for what we perceived to be justice— but in this fallen world, only anticipating the justice of a coming kingdom, what would God's will be? How would he answer? To what extent would he intervene?

Well-meaning friends from church were dogmatic: "God will give you those children," they said, speaking as it were for God. We weren't so sure. An adoptive home certainly seemed to us to be in the best interest of the children; it would shelter them from such significant, harmful, and unhealthy neglect. But wasn't the need for intervention through adoption proof that things on earth were not in harmony with God's will? In a world operating under the will of God, children would be sheltered and cared for by loving parents who bore them; there would be no need for adoption.

It is not surprising that theologians often talk of God's will in two ways: his *permissive* will and his *directive* will.

That which he allows and that which he intends and so causes to happen. Could we say, then, that a fallen world is his permissive will; a coming righteous kingdom his directive will?

So how would God answer this persistent prayer of ours? If, in this world, he *permitted* circumstances that made adoption a need, how could we be sure he would intervene, *directively*, just because we prayed? All around the globe, people—even godly people—faced hardship. History is the story of suffering often unchecked, of disaster only sometimes averted.

And for two years, at the bedside of a confused toddler, my wife and I prayed to this silent God whose will was now so mysterious, whose ways were now so perplexing. As a result of those months of intercession and with the eventual answer in mind, the Lord's Prayer took on a meaning to me it may not otherwise have had. I remember during that time drawing a cartoon in which a small face was cowering under the tent-like pages of an overturned Bible. The caption read: "Your will be done on earth as it is in heaven . . . just so it's heavenly." And I drew that because I knew, contrary to the encouragement of Christian friends, that God's will is not always bliss. What he permits on earth is not always "heavenly."

Not yet.

And that is why we pray: "Your kingdom come, your will be done on earth as it is in heaven."

Theologians have crossed swords over the question of the kingdom—what it is, what it isn't—but is it really that unclear? Jesus said, "Let the little children come to me, and do not hinder them, for the kingdom of God belongs to such as these. I tell you the truth, anyone who will not receive the kingdom of God like a little child will never enter it" (Mark 10:14–15). It must not be too confusing. In fact, "The knowledge of the secrets of the kingdom of God has been given to you," Jesus said (Luke 8:10). "But to others," he continued, "I speak in parables, so that 'though seeing, they may not see; though hearing, they may not understand.'"

To put it simply: The kingdom is where the king is. So, early in the gospels, the news is announced: "The kingdom of God is near you" (Luke 10:9). The kingdom was near because the king was near. And yet, though near, the kingdom was not a locality, not a province to be entered.

What happened after Jesus miraculously fed the five thousand? And how did Jesus react?

"Jesus, knowing that they intended to come and make him king by force, withdrew again to a mountain by himself" (John 6:15).

Had they succeeded, he would have failed. Jesus will accept kingship on his terms only, and those are not the terms of an earthly monarchy.

It has never been possible to enter the kingdom by crossing a border. The Gospels spoke of it as "hard to enter." A child could walk right in, but, said Jesus: "How hard it is for the rich to enter the kingdom of God! Indeed, it is easier for a camel to go through the eye of a needle than for a rich man to enter the kingdom of God" (Luke 18:24–25).

Where was this kingdom, then, that it would be accessible to the childlike and inaccessible to the self-sufficient? The clues lie in the parables Jesus used to describe the kingdom. He spoke of seeds and farmers, good soil and bad soil, birds and rocks and thorns; all to say that the kingdom was somehow related to how we heard God's word, how we accepted it and acted on it (Mark 4). It is not surprising, then, that the gospels speak of the kingdom of God being within us, because that is where the king intends to reign.

The kingdom is where the king is.

So it is that the apostle Paul would later speak of the kingdom of God with words that picture inner character traits and spiritual qualities. "The kingdom of God is not a matter of eating and drinking," he said, "but of righteousness, peace and joy in the Holy Spirit" (Romans 14:17). "The kingdom of God is not a matter of talk but of power" (1 Corinthians 4:20). And what is the kingdom's power if not the strength for internal change?

In fact, a significant change must overtake us before we can see the kingdom of God. "No one can see the kingdom of God unless he is born again," Jesus said (John 3:3). "Born of water and the Spirit" (3:5).

The kingdom is where the king is. And we could say that, in some sense at least, there are "places" the king refuses to be. Why? Because the kingdom of God is reserved for people who are fundamentally different. "Do you not know that the wicked will not inherit the kingdom of God? Do not be deceived: Neither the sexually immoral nor idolaters nor adulterers nor male prostitutes nor homosexual offenders nor thieves nor the greedy nor drunkards nor slanderers nor swindlers will inherit the kingdom of God" (1 Corinthians 6:9–10).

In contrast, he says, "That is what some of you were. But you were washed, you were sanctified, you were justified in the name of the Lord Jesus Christ and by the Spirit of our God" (verse 11). Through God's grace and our faith we are made worthy subjects of the king. As Paul states it elsewhere: "He has rescued us from the dominion of darkness and brought us into the kingdom of the Son he loves, in whom we have redemption, the forgiveness of sins" (Colossians 1:13–14).

But there is another dimension to the kingdom of God—a future dimension—beyond his spiritual rule now in the lives of his followers. Paul looks forward to the resurrection of the body and to changes that will sweep the universe. "The end will come, when [Christ] hands over the kingdom to God the Father after he has destroyed all dominion, authority and power" (1 Corinthians 15:24). Even death itself will be obliterated. And we will participate in this consummation of time and anguish, when all that is wrong will be made right. "Flesh and blood cannot inherit the kingdom of God," Paul says (verse 50). But we will be raised from the dead, changed and fit for an eternal kingdom. The Scriptures, therefore, speak of the kingdom as coming at some unexpected future time because the king himself is coming again. The kingdom is where the king is. And the day is coming—and soon—when all human history will be swallowed up in his endless reign.

So when I pray, "Your kingdom come," I am expressing my longing for his government. I am voicing my anticipation of a kingdom that puts an end to death and tears, sin and injustice. I am saying: "Lord, come now. Take control of all that is truly yours." But I am also affirming that I want to be under his authority now—until he comes, not just after he comes. I am saying: "Lord, don't delay. Rule me now. Master me, lead me, change me, and if you must, break me, that my will would bow to yours."

To pray, "Your kingdom come," submissively and with understanding, is also to express that next, inseparable phrase of the Lord's Prayer: "Your will be done on earth as it is in heaven." The ideas are parallel. "I want your kingdom, I crave your will."

Certainly, the prayer looks forward. We grow tired of lesser kingdoms and the corruption of the human will. We imagine what it would be like for the universe to be governed by his wise, kind and righteous will.

But, of course, just as his kingdom may come to us— within us—long before it is acknowledged by the world, so we may acquiesce to his will, long before "every knee should bow . . . and every tongue confess that Jesus Christ is Lord" (Philippians 2:10–11).

I pray the prayer today, impatient with the imperfect present, calling for the perfect future to come. But I pray, too, that the characteristics of the future would invade the present. When I pray, "Your will be done on earth as it is in heaven," I am saying: "I bend my will to yours. I will not argue with your will as it comes to me today. If you bring joy to me, I will celebrate. But even if you bring pain, I will trust you and love you."

In this, we follow the example of the king himself who rules us. "When Christ came into the world, he said [to the Father]: ... 'Here I am.... I have come to do your will, O God'" (Hebrews 10:5, 7). He said that, even though it led to unimaginable pain. His submission culminated in a lonely prayer, the night of his arrest: "My Father," he said, "if it is not possible for this cup to be taken away unless I drink it, may your will be done" (Matthew 26:42).

Until the kingdom does come, until all earth bows to the king's will, God's will for us may sometimes bring pain, as the king himself faced pain. This is the cost of the prayer we cannot lightly pray: "Your will be done. I submit regardless."

And so, one December morning, my wife and I sat in a cold, impersonal judicial chamber, awaiting the decision of human will. Yet, because we had prayed and because we were citizens of a greater kingdom, we knew higher powers were at work. God's will would be done, even though we could not presume to know what that would mean.

Even though he was silent.

That was sixteen years ago. Our oldest son is now on his own, facing the challenges of a world at odds with the will of God. From time to time I still pray for the welfare of his sister, the daughter I have never known.

We fix our eyes not on what is seen, but on what is unseen.
For what is seen is temporary, but what is unseen is eternal.
2 Corinthians 4:18

 Sixteen
Faith:
Beyond the Shadow of Doubt

Though I never knew him, my mother's twin brother was my introduction to doubt, long before I embraced faith. He was the subject of unanswered prayer, long before I found answers. He was, it seemed, the object of Heaven's coldness, long before I discovered the warmth of God's love.

Carl died at seventeen, electrocuted in a freak accident. He lingered briefly, comatose, in the sterile world of a hospital in Topeka, Kansas. And as he lay, suspended between death and life, his brothers and sisters prayed for him, clawing to find shreds of faith to hold on to. But he died.

Years later, my mother would often voice her memories. She told me how she had prayed that Carl would live. And she told me how her mother had finally returned from the hospital one day with the news: Carl would not be coming home.

"But I prayed," my mother said weakly. "I prayed that he would live."

And Grandma had startled her with the confession: "I prayed that he would not live." Had Carl "lived," he would have been incapable of life. Even before he died, that great jolt

133

to his system had done its irreversible work. And Grandma could not bear to see her son live on in such death.

And so my mother wrestled with doubt and faith, with unanswered and answered prayer, with Heaven's coldness and Heaven's warmth.

With God's silence.

Christians don't generally set out to doubt God, to call the essence of their faith into question. For most of us, life's pain simply catches us off guard; the reality of hardship trips us up. Doubt overtakes us in the race of faith because earth's suffering screams in our ears, distracting us—sometimes to the point that the race itself seems altogether meaningless. If faith cannot reasonably address hurt, what good is it?

If faith is so short on resources that its only answer to suffering is to ignore it, it is pointless. Honest people would choose honest doubt over dishonest faith. Brave people would say, "I must face earth's pain in all its intensity. I must not run from it. And if faith is merely an anesthetic to cover up the pain without honestly confronting it, doubt has more integrity."

A lot has happened to me since I first heard my mother talk about her pain for Carl. Childhood curiosity about doubt and faith and prayer and Heaven turned first to smoldering questions and then to occasional flare-ups of doubt. But in late adolescence and into early adulthood I found a sturdy and growing faith in Christ that has enabled me to face hardship—honestly, I think—while still holding on to God. I have found this possible because God's Word faces pain honestly, without the empty anesthetic of bright, cheery words to cover it up.

In admitting the reality of life's pain, God has given us less to doubt. He has answered our greatest questions (in frustratingly general terms, at least), so that he can now say to us, as he said to Thomas the sincere doubter, "Blessed are those who have not seen and yet have believed" (John 20:29).

Still, life hurts us and doubt plagues us. We have heard Christ say, "You do not want to leave me too, do you?" (John 6:67). And we have answered, "Lord, to whom shall we go? You have the words of eternal life. We believe and know that you are the Holy One of God" (John 6:68–69). But now something as small as a question mark wedges between us and our God. A fissure develops. A crack opens.

Where can we turn? We have ruled out all other options to follow Christ alone. Then our doubt asks, "Is Christ enough?"

How then can we who live by faith make sense out of doubt? Here are some guidelines I have found helpful.

❦

Consider whose company you're keeping. There's something sinister about the quiet way doubt eats at us, bringing shame, and a reluctance to admit its presence. Great faith we're proud of, but who boldly owns up to doubt? Who tarnishes his own halo by confessing weakness of faith? Who says, "Pray for me; I question God"?

Yet consider Job, a man God called "blameless and upright" (Job 1:8). Doubt gnawed at him.

"God has wronged me and drawn his net around me. Though I cry, 'I've been wronged!' I get no response; though I call for help, there is no justice. He has blocked my way so I cannot pass; he has shrouded my paths in darkness. He has stripped me of my honor and removed the crown from my head. He tears me down on every side till I am gone; he uproots my hope like a tree. His anger burns against me; he counts me among his enemies" (Job 19:6–11).

Job sank deep into doubt and despair. Should we be ashamed to be classified with Job as people capable of doubt?

Consider the lament of Jeremiah, "the weeping prophet," set apart to speak for God even before his birth (Jeremiah 1:5).

"[God] has walled me in so I cannot escape; he has weighed me down with chains. Even when I call out or cry for help, he shuts out my prayer. He has barred my way with blocks of stone; he has made my paths crooked" (Lamentations 3:7–9).

Jeremiah wondered, did God tune in to his prayers? We may often wonder the same.

Consider Jesus in Gethsemane. His agony. His emotional distress.

"He took Peter, James and John along with him, and he began to be deeply distressed and troubled. 'My soul is overwhelmed with sorrow to the point of death,' he said to them. 'Stay here and keep watch.'

"Going a little farther, he fell to the ground and prayed that if possible the hour might pass from him. 'Abba, Father,' he said, 'everything is possible for you. Take this cup from me. Yet not what I will, but what you will'" (Mark 14:33–36).

Consider Jesus at Golgotha. His desperate aloneness. "My God, my God, why have you forsaken me?" (Mark 15:34).

God understands, better than we can imagine, our feelings of panic in the face of suffering. God understands doubt; his choice servants have experienced it. God understands questions that would drive us to plead with him to change life's agenda; his own Son voiced such a question.

Yet in the midst of Job's great struggle of doubt, he did find a measure of faith:

"I know that my Redeemer lives, and that in the end he will stand upon the earth. And after my skin has been destroyed, yet in my flesh I will see God" (Job 19:25–26).

Jeremiah faced his nation's devastation, yet found faith to pronounce:

"Because of the LORD's great love we are not consumed, for his compassions never fail. They are new every morning;

great is your faithfulness. I say to myself, 'The LORD is my portion; therefore I will wait for him'" (Lamentations 3:22–24).

Jesus willingly—though not without pleading for an alternative—submitted to his Father's will. Similarly, we may feel encumbered with crushing doubt, yet find, somewhere within, a flicker of faith, however faint. This was Paul's experience. "We are hard pressed on every side," he said, "but not crushed; perplexed, but not in despair" (2 Corinthians 4:8).

When my doubt sparks guilt, I remember I am not alone. I am, in fact, in good company.

Determine the source of your doubt. There are different breeds of doubt. I have chosen to emphasize here the doubt that is triggered by hardship and suffering—by the effort to make faith fit with the painful realities of life. This is what forces the question for most of us. Someone we love died. Children face hunger. We are crippled by disease. We lose a job. Or a marriage. Now what does faith mean? And we scramble to hold back our doubts as life assails faith. Doubt, then, can come from pain.

Doubt may also rise from legitimate intellectual questions. We read the Bible and find ideas that seem, at least, contradictory. Genesis 1 does not seem to square with Genesis 2. We mentally chart the miracles of Christ and find one blind beggar in one gospel and two in another. We stumble over evolution and creation. We find the Virgin Birth questionable. We may be honest in our quest for faith, but we are not prepared to squelch reasonable questions. And doubts surface in our thinking.

Doubt may also spring from unbelief. This may sound oddly redundant, but doubt and unbelief are not necessarily the same. Sometimes our doubt is faith staggering for firm footing. Sometimes, though, it is mutiny against faith itself. In the first case, we are like the man who said to Jesus, "I do believe; help me overcome my unbelief!" (Mark 9:24). In the second, we are like unbelieving Israel of whom it was said, "The message they heard was of no value to them, because those who heard did not combine it with faith" (Hebrews 4:2). Doubt, then, grows out of determined disbelief.

Whether consciously or subconsciously, we sometimes use doubt to rationalize disobedience. We face the hard words of Scripture and their demands on us, and suddenly we are not quite sure of our faith. Coincidence? Is this honest doubt, then, or simply sin embellished and adorned? This form of doubt may resemble intellectual questioning; in fact, it is simply disbelief.

Hebrews cautions that "no one . . . fall by following [Israel's] example of disobedience," then reminds us: "The word of God is living and active. Sharper than any double-edged sword, it penetrates even to dividing soul and spirit, joints and marrow; it judges the thoughts and attitudes of the heart. Nothing in all creation is hidden from God's sight. Everything is uncovered and laid bare before the eyes of him to whom we must give account" (Hebrews 4:11–13).

When doubt takes hold of us we need to ask ourselves where the questions are coming from. Are we covering sinfulness with a coat of "doubt"? Are we using doubt as an excuse to resist God's work within us? Will we bring these doubts, and our motives, under the scrutiny of Scripture?

Doubt surfaces in our thinking. Intellectual questions call for reasonable answers. How willing are we to read and study open-mindedly? Are we open to efforts at reconciling faith and thought?

Doubt erupts, almost reflexively, from our pain. Will we bring our questions to a God who hurts with us, even if we must wait for satisfying answers?

Where are the doubts coming from? It makes a difference.

Accept that faith is still under construction. My mother had already stood at her father's grave by the time her seventeen-year-old brother died. Certainly Carl's death had prompted some questions about God. Yet, years later, she was daily at the bedside of Marian, a close friend who was nearing death. The cancer had seemed so capricious. Indiscriminate. Why Marian?

And Marian's faith wavered. What memories stirred in my mother's mind when Marian expressed doubt? When she questioned God's love? What did my mother think when Marian's young daughter said, "I don't understand. I prayed for Mommy to get well and she didn't"?

I'm not sure how it happened, but my mother had made peace with her questions. She was emotionally free to stand by a friend in her doubt. I do not think that the questions, for her, were resolved. I do not think she was free from doubt. But it was less binding than it had been.

Faith and doubt are not opposite sides of the same line—stand on the faith side or stand on the doubt side. Faith is something we grow into; doubt is something we grow out of. Gradually. And the movement is not always forward—out of doubt, into faith.

As we picture a partially filled cup, we sometimes speculate: Is the cup half full, or half empty? If we see faith as the contents of the cup, is it half full of faith, or half full of doubt? And if we look at the cup—our experience—and see one-half doubt, is doubt all we see?

As God looks at the half-full, half-empty cup, what does he see? The doubt? Or the faith? Or, switching analogies, if faith is merely a tiny seed—say, a mustard seed—can God see it? Is he moved by it? Or is he too busy gazing at the ample doubt that may surround that speck of faith?

We know the answer: God sees such faith. And is moved.

Had we encountered Gideon hiding in the winepress or tearing down the altar to Baal under cover of darkness, would we have hailed him: "Mighty Man of Faith!" or "Weakling of Doubt"? Hebrews 11 includes him in the catalog of people of faith.

What did God see?

Faith in process.

Doubt may be part of faith's process, then. It may be faith, grasping at life—at life's worst, trying to force faith and life to agree. This scuffle between faith and life we call doubt. Sometimes it is, more accurately, faith reaching. Growing. If there is a flicker of faith anywhere, the cup is half full, not half empty.

But let us not accept doubt too easily. I have read too many books and heard too many messages that seem to hold up doubt as a virtue. We grant that doubt is commonplace. We grant that it is not necessarily sin. We grant that it is a process. But, though honesty is a virtue, doubt is not. We must not rewrite Hebrews 11, substituting doubt for faith. Faith is the substance of things hoped for; doubt is, at best, the shadow.

"We live by faith, not by sight" (2 Corinthians 5:7). Faith is the virtue, not doubt. "Blessed are those who have not seen and yet have believed" (John 20:29).

Nurture a forever perspective. Certain Scriptures seem particularly magnetized with startling ideas. As I have pondered faith and doubt, I have often been attracted to 2 Corinthians. In the eleventh chapter Paul contrasts his experiences with those of the false apostles. The chapter builds to this climax:

"I have worked much harder, been in prison more frequently, been flogged more severely, and been exposed to death again and again. Five times I received from the Jews the forty lashes minus one. Three times I was beaten with rods, once I was stoned, three times I was shipwrecked, I spent a night and a day in the open sea. I have been constantly on the move. I have been in danger from rivers, in danger from bandits, in danger from my own countrymen, in danger from Gentiles; in danger in the city, in danger in the country, in danger at sea; and in danger from false brothers. I have labored and toiled and have often gone without sleep; I have known hunger and thirst and have often gone without food; I have been cold and naked. Besides everything else, I face daily the pressure of my concern for all the churches. Who is weak, and I do not feel weak? Who is led into sin, and I do not inwardly burn?" (verses 23–29).

How could Paul go on? Why wasn't he paralyzed by doubt? The same book—2 Corinthians—gives the clue.

"We do not lose heart. Though outwardly we are wasting away, yet inwardly we are being renewed day by day. For our light and momentary troubles are achieving for us an eternal glory that far outweighs them all. So we fix our eyes not on what is seen, but on what is unseen. For what is seen is temporary, but what is unseen is eternal" (2 Corinthians 4:16–18).

What kept Paul going?

Perspective.

Life is perplexing. God tolerates, on his planet, so much that is hideous. Holocaust and Hiroshima. Abortion and incest. Hunger and disease. Disaster and violence. Death. In life as we know it, pain is inescapable. Surrounded by our contemporary comforts, we may deftly sidestep the questions for some time. But sooner or later, reality forces the point. How can we help but be swallowed up with doubt? How can anyone go on?

Perspective.

There is more. This life is not all. God will right all wrongs. He is not indifferent. He is not powerless. He is waiting. And if, in the meantime, we sometimes seem preoccupied with doubt, perhaps it is prompted more by impatience than outright disbelief.

I never knew my uncle, but because he lived—and died—I learned of doubt and faith, of unanswered and answered prayer, of Heaven's coldness and Heaven's warmth. I learned of the silence of God. Carl, my unknown uncle, was merely the introduction to questions life has raised repeatedly since my childhood.

I am now convinced that Heaven is warm and friendly, not cold and indifferent. I am convinced my prayers are heard and answered, not ignored and forgotten. I firmly believe God is speaking, even through his silence. I have found faith fixed on Christ, growing stronger year after year, though still, doubts at times persist.

I am, quite simply, impatient for better things.

But now, how strong is faith?

In the face of the silence of God, can it carry us through the worst that life might bring?

Can it sustain us through the greatest of our fears?

My days are like the evening shadow;
I wither away like grass.
But you, O Lord, sit enthroned forever;
your renown endures through all generations.
You will arise and have compassion.
Psalm 102:11–13

Seventeen
Fear: Ultimate Test of Trust

Endless must be our terror until we come heart to heart
with the fire-core of the universe, the first and the last
of the living One.
George MacDonald

I have tried to reconstruct my earliest recollection of
fear and must confess that it has been somewhat difficult. I
do recall, however, one early incident that should have triggered fear but did not. I was no older than four, and my dad,
a quartermaster in the United States Navy, was stationed in
Adak, Alaska, on the Aleutian Islands. He had the day off,
and the family was out exploring that barren island. I
remember straying from my folks, probably no more than a
few yards. But it was far enough. I walked to the edge of a
cliff—I am not sure now how far it might have been to the
bottom; at the time it seemed miles high. I was curious and
fascinated, and methodically inched my toes closer and closer

to the edge, trying to place them right on that neat dividing line between rock and air. I had no sense of danger.

What happened next happened quickly.

Someone said, "Where's Jimmy?" My mother gasped as she saw my danger. And strong arms lifted me off my feet, pulled me away from the edge, and hauled me off to be confined to the car.

My father intervened.

As I sit here, reflecting on fear, it strikes me how like my father God is. He sees us in our danger (whether we do or not) and so often intervenes, securing our safety.

As King David expressed it: "[The Lord] redeems [my] life from the pit and crowns [me] with love and compassion" (Psalm 103:4).

With a God like that, what is there to fear?

On the other hand, as my eyes scan left across my open Bible from Psalm 103 to Psalm 102, they fall on these words: "My days vanish like smoke; my bones burn like glowing embers. My heart is blighted and withered like grass; I forget to eat my food. Because of my loud groaning I am reduced to skin and bones. . . . All day long my enemies taunt me; those who rail against me use my name as a curse. For I eat ashes as my food and mingle my drink with tears because of your great wrath, for you have taken me up and thrown me aside. My days are like the evening shadow; I wither away like grass" (verses 3–5, 8–11).

My life redeemed from the pit. My enemies taunt me.

Nothing to fear. Inescapable fear.

Scripture chronicles both: cause to trust and reason to fear.

There is, of course, much to fear. Those who follow current events know that. And with so much to fear, so many potential dangers, it is natural to ask, Where is God? Scripture is filled with the question, as is our experience.

Yet here I must confess annoyance that we affluent American Christians seem slow to embrace that balance of trust and fear. We tend to cope with worldwide heartache (or the grief of a neighbor) by pushing it aside. We seem prone to downplay hardship and understandable fearfulness; quick to quote Psalm 103 in our experience, slow to see Psalm 102 in the experience of others.

In times of apprehension, one hymn has repeatedly come to my mind: "Great Is Thy Faithfulness." It is often a hymn of choice at memorial services as well as festivals of Thanksgiving. It is an unexcelled expression of confidence in the goodness of God.

I recall my surprise when I discovered that that great hymn was drawn directly from the third chapter of Lamentations. As I read the prophet, my eyes fell on this pronouncement of the goodness of God—an island of hope amid deep and terrifying experiences. The chapter opens with words like these: "I am the man who has seen affliction" (verse 1); it moves toward conclusion, framing these thoughts: "We have suffered terror and pitfalls, ruin and destruction" (verse 47). Between the two: "Because of the Lord's great love we are not consumed, for his compassions never fail. They are new every morning; great is your faithfulness" (verses 22–23). For many, this dizzying swing from hardship to hopefulness, from fear to God's faithfulness, is precisely the reality of life.

Others of us have lived a rather buffered existence, insulated from pain. We may feel that our faith is a shield not only against Satan's flaming arrows of spiritual assault, but against life's terrifying times of sickness, accident, or violence. We cling to out-of-context Bible verses as promise of protection or prosperity, while three-fourths of the world must settle for definitions of "comfort" and "safety" quite different from our own. For many of us, blessing means success; spirituality means prosperity; fear means nothing. Not so much because of some guarantee of God's intervention—not really—but because of the privilege of American birth.

We enjoy smooth sailing through life not because of our strong faith, but because, in the providence of God, hardship has so rarely rocked our boat.

Some Christians have fared differently. They have learned through fearful experience that we live, for now, in a fallen world. And a silent God does not always preserve us from harm.

I remember a young guy who had been in a college Sunday school class I taught, a gifted cellist. He had just moved from Chicago to Atlanta with his new wife, where he had taken a job with an automobile dealership to cover expenses as he continued his music studies and nationwide performance. He had been out on the road, test-driving a car with a customer, when the man pulled a gun on him, forced him from the car, and took his life. I recall the shock when we heard of his murder. A wave of empathy swept over me as I imagined the terror he must have felt in those few moments before he was shot. And I wondered what word Christ might have that could possibly quell such fear, to say nothing of comforting his young wife left behind.

He was a Christian.

He trusted God.

But there was no intervention for him.

The same emotions gripped me several years later when I received news of a similar ordeal a friend's daughter endured. But for some reason, this second brush with violence and vicarious fear brought to mind words of Jesus that ever since have been to me an odd source of solace and strength. I say "odd," because these are not sweet, soft words. They are hard, angular words, laced with irony.

"I tell you, my friends, do not be afraid of those who kill the body and after that can do no more. But I will show you whom you should fear: Fear him who, after the killing of the body, has power to throw you into hell. Yes, I tell you, fear him" (Luke 12:4–5).

Do not fear? Do not be afraid of those who kill the body and after that can do no more? After the killing of the body, what's left?

Far, far more than we can begin to imagine.

Beyond the killing of the body lies the unending reach of eternity. Beyond the killing of the body lies the undiminished comfort, or condemnation, of a holy God. Beyond the killing of the body lies the end of earth-bound fear and the beginning of unimaginable hope or unparalleled terror. Beyond the killing of the body lies the beginning.

The point, of course, is that a healthy fear of God puts human fear in perspective; and perspective is what we need when fear faces us. In fact, standing in the presence of sickness, accident, even violence, when we are stripped of all earthly hope, nothing can blunt the edge of our apprehension except a clear view of the face of God.

I used to wonder how martyrs could possibly endure not death so much as the prospect of impending death. The horror of knowing that the worst was about to happen. At that absolute edge of human experience, what could sustain a person?

A clear view of the face of God.

I have had friends who have received word of terminal illness and somehow found grace that carried them through the trauma, right to the end. Not without struggles, questions, doubts, or fear. But also not without grace. When fears rose up, what battled them into subservience?

A clear view of the face of God.

We cannot handle fear as long as it is a wall we cannot break through, closing in on us. But if we can see past that fear, if we can look through it into the face of God, if we can perceive eternity overlapping today, then that perspective can hold us up, regardless of what we endure.

Exactly what, then, is a clear view of the face of God? And how do we bring it into focus?

Stephen, of course, provides a very literal and instructive picture in Acts 7. As he faced his martyrdom, heaven opened to receive him.

> Stephen, full of the Holy Spirit, looked up to heaven and saw the glory of God, and Jesus standing at the right hand of God. "Look," he said, "I see heaven open and the Son of Man standing at the right hand of God."
>
> At this they covered their ears and, yelling at the top of their voices, they all rushed at him, dragging him out of the city and began to stone him. Meanwhile, the witnesses laid their clothes at the feet of a young man named Saul.
>
> While they were stoning him, Stephen prayed, "Lord Jesus, receive my spirit." Then he fell on his knees and cried out, "Lord, do not hold this sin against them." When he had said this, he fell asleep." (verses 55–60)

What sustained Stephen, we could conclude, was a literal clear view of the face of God—a gift to him, I gather, at his point of need, from the Holy Spirit. Yet this vision was not something he was seeking or anticipating; rather, he seemed surprised as it materialized before him. The point I draw from Stephen's experience is this: he had a clear view of the face of God long before his eyes were opened to see what his enemies could not see—the glory of heaven.

Why do I say that? Follow Stephen through Acts 6 and 7, through the events leading up to his death. The Jerusalem church, already numbering in the thousands, was looking for seven exemplary men, "known to be full of the Spirit and wisdom" (6:3), to oversee the distribution of food to widows. Stephen was singled out from among the hundreds of possible choices, a man "full of faith and of the Holy Spirit" (6:5). As the narrative unfolds, Stephen is further described as a man "full of God's grace and power," a man who "did great wonders and miraculous signs among the people" (6:8).

Opposition arose against Stephen, but the arguments against him failed, because "they could not stand up against his wisdom or the Spirit by whom he spoke" (6:10). So as false charges had been brought against Jesus, false charges were brought against Stephen also, and he was dragged before the authorities. But as they looked intently on him, "they saw that his face was like the face of an angel" (6:15).

The charges against him were voiced, and he stood to make his defense. But what was his defense? A recitation of holy history, the movement of a nation away from God, the loving overture of that God for his people, climaxing in the rejected gift of the Christ. And this man—full of the Spirit and wisdom, full of faith and the Holy Spirit, full of God's grace and power—looked past his fearful circumstances, across the landscape of eternity, and into the face of God.

Maybe at our moment of greatest fear, the Spirit will open our eyes to see the glory of heaven, literally. It has happened before. But it is our grasp of God's loving character and our perception of his hand in history that bring our first glimpse of his face. It is the Spirit and wisdom and faith and grace that first open our eyes, so that in our times of fear, we perceive the face of God.

Consider Paul's fearful experience. "We were under great pressure, far beyond our ability to endure, so that we despaired even of life. Indeed, in our hearts we felt the sentence of death. But this happened that we might not rely on ourselves but on God, who raises the dead" (2 Corinthians 1:8–9).

"We are hard pressed on every side, but not crushed; perplexed, but not in despair; persecuted, but not abandoned; struck down, but not destroyed" (4:8–9).

"We do not lose heart. Though outwardly we are wasting away, yet inwardly we are being renewed day by day. For our light and momentary troubles are achieving for us an eternal glory that far outweighs them all. So we fix our eyes not on what is seen but on what is unseen. For what is seen is temporary, but what is unseen is eternal" (4:16–18).

His summary: "We live by faith, not by sight" (5:7).

With this backdrop, then, I reiterate the oddly comforting, fear-fighting words of Jesus: "I tell you, my friends, do not be afraid of those who kill the body and after that can do no more. But I will show you whom you should fear: Fear him who, after the killing of the body, has power to throw you into hell. Yes, I tell you, fear him" (Luke 12:4–5).

A healthy fear of God, a faith-recognition of who he is—"the fire-core of the universe, the first and the last of the living One"—puts human fear in perspective.

The fear of God as a source of comfort takes on greater forcefulness when those verses are considered in their context; for the words that surround them affirm the sovereignty and providence of our God.

All our experiences are seen and heard by our caring God. Jesus had just told his friends, "There is nothing concealed that will not be disclosed, or hidden that will not be made known. What you have said in the dark will be heard in the daylight, and what you have whispered in the ear in the inner rooms will be proclaimed from the roofs. I tell you, my friends, do not be afraid" (Luke 12:2–4).

The parallel passage in Matthew 10, as Jesus sent out his twelve disciples, foreshadows the reality of martyrdom and climaxes with these words: "What I tell you in the dark, speak in the daylight; what is whispered in your ear, proclaim from the roofs. Do not be afraid" (10:27–28).

Cross-reference this with the experiences of Paul and Stephen. Or with our own fearful trials.

Nothing is hidden from the eyes and ears of our caring God. And it is not stretching the point to say this: when the doctor whispers bad news in your ear, it is heard by God. Or, when you are threatened with violence in the dark, God knows, sees, hears, cares.

We are not forgotten. Jesus' words on fear, murder and hell were followed not by promise of deliverance, but by this simple assurance: "Are not five sparrows sold for two pennies? Yet not one of them is forgotten by God. Indeed, the very hairs of your head are all numbered. Don't be afraid; you are worth more than many sparrows" (Luke 12:6–7).

Psalm 103 expressed it: "[The Lord] redeems my life from the pit and crowns me with love and compassion" (verse 4). But even Psalm 102 moves past apprehension. "My days are like the evening shadow; I wither away like grass," the writer says, voicing his fear. Then he adds: "But you, O Lord, sit enthroned forever; your renown endures through all generations. You will arise and have compassion" (verses 11–13).

I wish I could say that the sheer strength of Bible study has freed me from fear. Such is not the case. But it is beginning to change my perspective. I do not know God's will for my earth-life, as I stand at the edge of all my fears. Perhaps at the final, seemingly irreversible second, his strong arms will lift me off my feet and pull me away from the danger. But even if he doesn't, even if I were to be hurled over the edge of the worst of my fears, I know I will land in his strong arms.

My blurred vision is beginning to clear, and the image I see is surely the face of God.

The eyes of the Lord are on the righteous and his ears
are attentive to their prayer.
1 Peter 3:12

This is the confidence we have in approaching God:
that if we ask anything according to his will, he hears us.
1 John 5:14

Eighteen
Prayer: Monologues with God?

As a new Christian, I was intrigued by the mechanics of
prayer. In those early months, I spent several weeks on a
ministry trip with a group of Christians more mature than I;
they were like older brothers and sisters to me. As we
prayed together, which we did three or four times a day,
their prayers seemed so much more impressive than my
own. I noticed there was a vocabulary to the initiated I was
yet to grasp. My more experienced friends sounded so
pious, and when someone made a particularly good point as
we prayed aloud, it sometimes triggered a chorus of "Amens"
or "Yes, Lords" from the others.

My own prayers, in contrast, were at first primitive and
straightforward; they were ideas, questions, or requests
more or less blurted out, with awkward intros or trailers
fashioned from the religion words I was starting to absorb.
If I prayed aloud with the group and somebody would second my motion with an "Amen" or a "Yes, Lord," I became

distracted with the quiet thrill of having been accepted by them, and, flustered, I would lose my place in the prayer. During those weeks, I listened carefully, straining to pick up all the right phrases to incorporate into my devotional expression, and I knew I was making progress as I noted the others amen-ing my fledgling eloquence more frequently.

One afternoon about halfway through our weeks together, I had occasion to pray alone with our team leader, Stan, who was four years my senior. I looked up to him as a model of all I wanted to become in a Christian: serious yet witty; sensitive yet confident. And paramountly, most devout. Stan prayed first that afternoon, beautifully and at some length, as I cheered him on, so to speak, with a sprinkling of those murmurs of affirmation I had picked up from my praying friends. Stan would express a concern to God, and I would "Yes, Lord" it with the precise intonation I had heard so many times from him. He would applaud the majesty or kindness of God, and I would punctuate his sentence for him with a heartfelt "Amen."

After a while, Stan apparently ran out of things to say and fell silent. I picked up the slack with the host of legitimate concerns that were on my mind. After praying for a while, a sudden ambivalence washed over me, eroding my concentration. I knew I was sounding good, but I now noticed that Stan wasn't affirming me with even an occasional "Amen" or "Yes, Lord." Not a single sanctified grunt of agreement. What was I doing wrong?

I paused. And that's when I heard it. Stan was snoring!

Irritated, I stopped praying mid-sentence, got up and left the room. Why pray if no one was listening to me anyhow!

I had stepped out of the room, closed the door quietly behind me, and flopped on the couch in the living room before I realized what I was doing. *Why pray if no one was listening to me anyhow?* Who had been my audience when I bowed my head and opened my mouth? Stan?

The next morning I rose early, showered, and went for a long walk alone. As I trudged along, I began speaking to God, at first silently and embarrassed to own my pride, but the longer I walked, the more conversational I became until at last I realized that I had been speaking to God aloud for some time. It was a remarkable and rare experience that gave me a hint of what prayer could become. I returned to the house, and to my friends, determined that I would say nothing of my conversation that morning, for it was too personal, and was exclusively mine, not theirs.

Those two back-to-back experiences years ago—one negative, the other positive—introduced me to what I have concluded is the essence of every controversy about prayer. Behind every complaint or question is the greater issue: Who is my audience? Whom am I talking to when I pray?

I know the question may not be particularly relevant to everyone. There are those who would argue that prayer has great benefit to the person praying even if *no one* is listening. Prayer has a certain therapeutic quality. The path to healing for many of our emotional problems is talk; something almost medicinal happens in the simple verbal expression of our feelings and concerns. Talk to a friend, a pastor, a counselor. Talk to God. You are more likely to find wellness through conversation, than if you clam up and cover your confusion or hurt or rage. Talk can be the psychological crowbar to leverage us out of hopelessness, particularly if faith promises brighter prospects. Talk can give perspective, help us organize our brain, process an array of options we ought to consider, even if we're "only talking to God."

Or think we are.

Of course, to many of us, this earthbound view of prayer is not fully satisfying. Is prayer merely psychological smoke and mirrors, just an illusion of something real that nevertheless benefits those who practice it? Or is prayer authentic? Who, in truth, is my audience? Whom am I talking to when I pray?

Let's be fair. For most people, even those of us who do pray, there are times when it just does not seem real. I stare at blankness, then talk to God as if conversing with a friend. But the conversation is one-sided. I babble to this cosmic friend who is, it seems, out of the room.

In contrast, I meet an acquaintance on the street. We stop to talk. I see him; I study his response. If something I say makes him uncomfortable, his expressions show it even before he speaks. If I flatter him ridiculously, he blushes. If I am incredibly witty, he smiles. If I have tragic news, he shares my grief. All of this before he even speaks.

But God never speaks. And I can never gauge his response visually. He does not fidget as if bored. He does not laugh as if amused. He does not cry as if sharing my sorrow. With God, if I believe my eyes and my ears, I am consigned to a one-sided conversation—a monologue.

But should I believe my eyes and ears?

To be sure, we do learn ways to explain away God's silence, his slowness, and his denial of our requests, but are the explanations true? Or are they just rationalizations to enable us to hold on to a faith that, terrifyingly, might be misplaced after all?

If I trust my limited, physical senses, if I consider prayer on the human level only, the idea of conversation with God would seem preposterous. But if God exists at all, we are not operating on the human level anyway.

An Old Testament story comes to mind which reminds us that with God, there is always more than meets the human eye.

Animosity arose between the king of Aram and the nation of Israel, but whenever Aram's king planned to attack Israel, the prophet Elisha was alerted by God and passed on the warning to Israel's king. Finally, exasperated, Aram's forces surrounded Elisha in the city of Dothan, much to the consternation of Elisha's servant.

"Oh, my lord," he said, "what shall we do?"

It was a calm Elisha that reassured his friend with an explanation that defied the empirical evidence. "Don't be afraid. Those who are with us are more than those who are with them."

Then Elisha prayed, "O Lord, open his eyes so he may see." The Old Testament reports that God answered Elisha's prayer. "The Lord opened the servant's eyes, and he looked and saw the hills full of horses and chariots of fire all around Elisha" (2 Kings 6).

I'm sure that servant came away from the encounter questioning the reliability of his five physical senses. As reliable as they may be in the physical realm, they just didn't go far enough. They were too limited. It is safe and wise to assume the same of ours. We don't see God, we don't hear his voice. That does not mean he is absent or incommunicado.

Who, then, is my audience if I look beyond what I can see? Whom am I talking to when I pray?

Faith says my companion in this conversation is a personal God who hears and cares. "Without faith it is impossible to please God," Scripture says. "Anyone who comes to him must believe that he exists and that he rewards those who earnestly seek him" (Hebrews 11:6). Faith opens up a way of perceiving things that not only supersedes my limited physical senses, but is in some way counter to them. "We live by faith," Scripture asserts, "not by sight" (2 Corinthians 5:7).

"'No eye has seen, no ear has heard, no mind has conceived what God has prepared for those who love him'—but God has revealed it to us by his Spirit" (1 Corinthians 2:9–10).

With words such as these in mind, why should anyone be surprised if prayer is not like a street-corner conversation? The issues we deal with go deeper than the weather or the performance of Wall Street's Dow Jones averages. In fact, these conversations with God can become so personal, or mystical, that we begin to feel the limits not only of our vocabulary, but of language itself. Faith introduces another realm and in that place, even the silence of God can become articulate.

We also have a largely untapped prayer resource in the gift of our imagination. I am amazed by the power of the human mind to invent and to devise solutions. But we also apply imagination's power in more pedestrian matters.

Most of us can flip through a catalog or glance at an advertisement and readily see ourselves driving that new car or enjoying that new furniture or sporting that new wardrobe. We can see it, through imagination's power. This imaginative capacity can be coddled and fed so that it creates unrestrained fantasy. The power of pornography is an extreme example.

That same imaginative capacity that is stroked by Madison Avenue or pampered in pornography can be released for good, if we will give it a theological education and harness it for prayer.

Why not imagine God as near you, walking with you, holding you? Scripture is filled with rich symbols of our caring God: a rock of protection, a caring shepherd, the living bread, a foundation for life. We could quite legitimately add our own very personal mental images. What is this God of the Bible like in our own experience? Imagine it! What would happen if we worked at prayer at least as earnestly as we worked at our catalogs and commercials? And what happens if we don't? It strikes me that prayer is much a product of what we bring to the process.

What would keep me from success in prayer, then? Well, unbelief would, because it would lead me to the wrong answer to the question, Who is my audience? Whom am I talking to when I pray?

Disinterest or distraction would also keep me from success in prayer, and there are many distractions. Hardship can distract me, if I am too preoccupied with my pain to converse with God. Success can distract me, if I am so self-assured that I feel no need to connect with the divine. Busyness can distract me, if I do not slow down enough to sort my values and prioritize my time.

Disgruntled with God, I can so easily call my occasional prayer empty and grouse about its ineffectiveness. What did it achieve? What did I gain from it? But if life has distracted me from a conscientious practice of the discipline of prayer, I am not qualified to judge it. How can I fairly evaluate the potential of prayer if I have not truly experienced it? And yet, if faith tells me that my audience is God, how can I let something or someone smaller than God distract me from the practice?

If I do not make the time to talk to God or if I am driven by wrong motives, I will not be successful in prayer. "You do not have," James says, "because you do not ask God. When you ask, you do not receive, because you ask with wrong motives, that you may spend what you get on your pleasures" (James 4:2–3). If God is my audience, if I know him for who he is, I will most naturally search out companionship with him, and what motivates him will, in time, transform my own motivations.

There are other problems with prayer, of course. Sometimes we do not find success because our perspective is so limited; we have no idea what to ask. Scripture repeatedly urges us to pray according to God's will, but what could be more mysterious than that? Yet the Bible seems to suggest that this God, who is our audience, also edits our sincere prayer so that it does conform to his will (Romans 8:26–27).

We can run through the usual complaints about prayer, then, catalog the problems, cross-reference them with appropriate and compelling Scripture, but our progress will be limited until we are convinced of the answer to the bigger question: Who is my audience? Who am I talking to when I pray?

At 28,000 feet, or thereabouts, en route from Orlando to Chicago, I experienced a turbulence that had nothing to do with my flight. For weeks, the spiritual waywardness and psychological garbage of a close friend of mine had weighed on my mind as it ought to have weighed on his. Yet his spiritual life was marked by duplicity, and his emotional problems had been stuffed so deep down inside for so long, he seemed neither capable nor interested in pulling them up and dealing with them. What contact he had with professional counselors had not yet been productive; his denial was simply too strong. Sitting there on that crammed 727, I prayed, but the prayer did not seem real; the conversation, after all, was one-sided. My mind wandered and I felt a twinge of guilt. This concern mattered to me; I believed God cared; why was it so hard to focus?

I reached for my carry-on, and pulled out a blue journal and began writing a letter to God. I was used to writing letters, addressing greeting or affirmation or concern to someone who could not give me immediate feedback as in a phone call or personal visit. As I wrote, I expressed my feelings of frustration, concern, powerlessness, anger. I reminded God of his love for my friend and his sovereign power to orchestrate circumstances in spite of the mystery of human willfulness. I asked God to make me prudent and balanced —to be a supportive friend, but not to interfere in the consequences of my friend's wrong behavior. And then, finally, after several pages and an hour of thought, I let it go. I could not change my friend, and I had no guarantee that God would manipulate circumstances to force spiritual compliance and psychological health. And yet, restfully, it was now out of my hands and in a grip more capable and loving than my own.

That letter-prayer felt like . . . what? A contract? The title deed to a problem? Perhaps this, but more personal and friendly. As I wrote that letter to God, I felt my frustration and helplessness flow out of me as certainly as the ink was flowing out of the pen.

Interestingly, there was a discernible point as I wrote when that letter to God ceased to be informing, ceased to be complaining, ceased to be pleading, and became instead simply companionship. I stopped writing and spent the last hour of the flight in quiet contemplation.

What happened within me on that afternoon flight from Florida to Illinois was parallel to my long early morning walk with God years before. A defining moment that transformed prayer. What I had wanted from prayer was action, results. What I needed was companionship.

I have noticed that the most intense prayer often rises out of the most hopeless, out-of-control, impossible circumstances, for it is these that show us our inadequacy, and drive us past petition and into companionship. Christ prayed an impossible prayer and found it a doorway to intimacy with his Father at a time when he critically needed it.

He prayed for a way out of the suffering he faced. "If it be possible," he said, "let this cup pass from me." This request the Father could not grant. "Nevertheless," Christ continued, "not my will, but yours be done."

In subservience to the Father's will, the request ended; the companionship did not, and Christ gained the strength he needed to face the inevitable ordeal.

Those moments of agony and helplessness provide a pattern for us. At times, we may be kept waiting; the Father may deny a request for good reasons we cannot fathom; we may be perplexed and despairing, but nothing can separate us from his love. It is because of such love that he is our willing and attentive audience, the one to whom we pray.

My interest in prayer now lies deeper than trying to figure out how to make it work for me so that I receive a payoff for my time and effort, so that I can get things out of God. My greater interest is in communication, and since God speaks the language of silence, all my talk, all my words, all my good requests may not necessarily be the end of prayer, but merely its beginning.

We are told, for instance, that Christ often prayed all night. Have you ever wondered about the details? What were those conversations like? Do we really suppose that it was nonstop talk? I'm not so sure.

I've seen it in friendship, I've experienced it in my marriage: some of the most sublime moments of companionship are moments shared in silence. Perhaps it can be the same with God. Perhaps an even deeper level of communication begins when we quit talking. Then, there in the silence, we both become articulate.

When I consider your heavens,
 the work of your fingers,
the moon and the stars,
 which you have set in place,
what is man that you are mindful of him,
 the son of man that you care for him?
Psalm 8:3–4

Nineteen
Quiet:
The Articulate Silence of God

"The present state of the world and the whole of life is diseased," Kierkegaard said. "If I were a doctor and were asked for my advice, I should reply, 'Create silence.'"

Create silence? Think of the effort so many of us put into resisting silence. Covering it up.

In our community there is a convent that encourages personal retreat, built around the discipline of silence. Some, of course, see its value and appreciate the opportunity. Others, I suspect, view the idea, if they give it any thought at all, as simply quaint, rather than powerful.

Isn't it remarkable, by contrast, that Jesus Christ's ministry grew out of six weeks of concentrated silence, and that he was sustained through the demands and stress of the next three years by that custom of his, those frequent all-night retreats into silence?

We might well view his baptism by John as the turning point, that public event that was to draw him into the maelstrom of prominence. But immediately following the commotion of public honor, "Jesus was led by the Spirit into the desert" (Matthew 4:1).

It was there—then—that he was tempted.

Matthew says of Jesus, "After fasting forty days and forty nights, he was hungry. The tempter came to him and said, 'If you are the Son of God, tell these stones to become bread'" (4:2–3). And on the drama goes: three representative temptations; three instructive responses. "Then the devil left him, and angels came and attended him" (4:11).

Mark relates the same sequence: the public recognition of his baptism, and then: "At once the Spirit sent him out into the desert, and he was in the desert forty days, being tempted by Satan. He was with the wild animals, and angels attended him" (1:12–13).

Luke concludes his account with these words: "When the devil had finished all these temptations, he left him until an opportune time. Jesus returned to Galilee in the power of the Spirit, and news about him spread through the whole countryside" (4:13–14).

Back into the noisy demands of the public eye.

But aren't you curious about those six weeks of silence? Forty solitary days? We know they weren't easy. He was hungry. He was harassed by Satan. Wild animals prowled about in the night. We might imagine he felt loneliness, as a foreshadowing of the abandonment he would later endure on the cross; Scripture does stress that angels ministered to him after, not during, the experience.

Six weeks of silence. Forty solitary days.

When he wasn't fending off attacks by Satan, what filled his quiet moments? Based on his habits as Scripture records them, we would assume he prayed. Shortly after his six weeks in the desert, Mark recounts, "Very early in the morning, while it was still dark, Jesus got up, left the house and went off to a solitary place, where he prayed" (1:35).

This flustered the busy, noisy disciples who, when they had found him, exclaimed, "Everyone is looking for you!" (1:37).

Not everyone.

His Father had already found him, and he had found his Father, in the silence of prayer.

It is fair to speculate that this also was his experience those forty days in the desert. Prayer.

It used to be when I read of Jesus and his all-night prayer vigils, I would imagine non-stop talk, and it intimidated me. At the time, I could pray for the missionaries around the world almost before you could say, "In Jesus' name, Amen." I now understand that if you are creative and thoughtful, the moments in prayer grow into a conversation in which it is easy to lose track of time. Even so, I'm not so sure the all-night prayer was non-stop talk, and I doubt Jesus talked himself hoarse those six weeks in the desert. I rather suspect he drew strength from the quiet companionship of God in silence.

Oddly, I have known Christians who feel a bit uneasy with such mystical talk of meditative silence. I guess it brings to mind mantras, emptied minds, and altered states. This is not my image of the silence of God and the silence of Christ.

Isn't it striking that when confronted by Satan, the first words out of the mouth of Christ were the words of God? Three times he quoted from Deuteronomy.

"Man does not live on bread alone, but on every word that comes from the mouth of God" (Deuteronomy 8:3).

"Do not put the Lord your God to the test" (6:16).

"Worship the Lord your God, and serve him only" (6:13).

Christ quoted Scripture so reflexively, because it was Scripture that filled his mind; and it was Scripture, and Christ's impressions of the character and ways of his Father, that filled his long hours of silence and made them articulate.

But Christ was not alone in experiencing such times of companionship and articulate silence. So many years before, God spoke to Abraham and sent him in search of a "city with foundations, whose architect and builder is God." He obeyed and went, "even though he did not know where he was going." God promised that from this one old man, "and he as good as dead," would come a nation, "descendants as numerous as the stars in the sky" (Hebrews 11:8–12).

And Abraham waited.

Can you see him on his journey, late into the night, as the fire's last glowing embers mirror a sky lit with a million stars? Can you see this man, who dared to act on belief, smiling in the darkness—in the silence—because he remembered a voice and a promise?

Years later, a shepherd boy, a descendant of Abraham, sat on a hillside under those same silent stars and quietly imagined what destiny might be his. Surely David carried with him the memory of those nights forever. Years later, remembering, he was overcome with his own smallness and his great God's concern.

"O LORD, our Lord, how majestic is your name in all the earth! . . . When I consider your heavens, the work of your fingers, the moon and the stars, which you have set in place, what is man that you are mindful of him, the son of man that you care for him?" (Psalm 8:1, 3–4).

Centuries pass, and a young girl is visited by an angel in the night. Her bewildered mind fills with wonder as she hears the words, "Do not be afraid, Mary, you have found favor with God" (Luke 1:30). When the Christ child is born, his mother—this spectator and participant in the miracle of the ages—listens, hushed, at the words of God from the mouths of shepherds. It is not surprising that throughout her silent moments, Mary "treasured up all these things and pondered them in her mind;" it is only surprising when we don't.

As I now write, it is the middle of the night and the house is silent. I can think of no more appropriate mood in which to conclude this book. I suppose for many writers, if their subject is of any consequence, they hope that the conclusion they write will in truth be an introduction. A beginning for those who read; a beginning also for the writer. We hope for words that make a difference.

And now I hope too for a silence that makes a difference. A silence we are pleased to create. For if the words of God will echo in our minds, whether we face the harshest of difficulties or "merely" the mystery of the ordinary, we will most surely find the silence of God to be articulate.

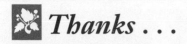 *Thanks . . .*

To Harriet, my wife, who reviewed the manuscript with me at every step and made insightful observations. I am indebted to her for her wisdom as well as her unselfish love.

To my son Michael, who was understanding and encouraging when I retreated to my study to read or pound on the computer keys. Thanks, Buddy.

To the following friends who read the manuscript and made valuable suggestions: Joy Bauerlein, Dr. Norm Ericson, Karen Johnson, Harold Myra, Marshall Shelley, Harold Smith, Dr. Dan Sommerville, Tim Stafford, and Dr. Herb Wolf.

To my friends at Zondervan, particularly Scott Bolinder and Bob Hudson, who have so greatly encouraged me.

To Susan Maycinik and her colleagues at *Discipleship Journal*, for granting me a forum to share many of the ideas found in the third section of the book.